美國華工田園生涯

梁靜源 著

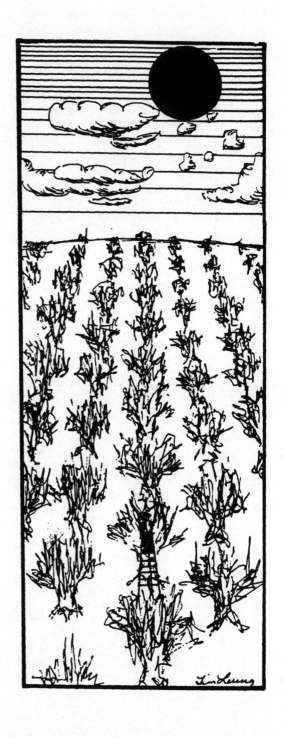

文史哲出版社印行

國立中央圖書館出版品預行編目資料

美國華工田園生涯 = One day, one dollar :
the Chinese farming experience in the
Sacramento River delta, California / 梁靜
源著. -- 初版. -- 臺北市：文史哲，民83
面 ； 公分
ISBN 957-547-840-1(平裝)

1. 華僑 - 美國 - 歷史

577.7252   83000080

美國華工田園生涯

著　者：梁　　　　靜　　　　源

出版者：文　史　哲　出　版　社

登記證字號：行政院新聞局局版臺業字五三三七號

發行人：彭　　　　正　　　　雄

發行所：文　史　哲　出　版　社

印刷者：文　史　哲　出　版　社

　　　台北市羅斯福路一段七十二巷四號
　　　郵撥〇五一二八八一二彭正雄帳戶
　　　電話：三　五　一　一　〇　二　八

實價新台幣三二〇元

中華民國八十三年四月初版

美國華工田園生涯　目　錄

目　錄

一

序言

加州的歷史可說是不同種族的歷史，不同國籍者先後定居加州，關於他們移居的原由、生活狀況及對加州發展的影響等，均有不少記載，華人也是最早到達加州者之一，他們參與始於一八四九年的尋金熱，此後十年間，華人與橫越大陸的鐵道工程結下不解之緣，並且在漁業、製衣、製煙（雪茄）、洗衣、家務、木材、築堤及農業方面，都扮演了重要角色。三藩市華埠雖是加州最大華埠，但華人也散居其他各州。在肥沃沙加緬度三角洲上，華埠中之樂居埠曾盛極一時，享譽達半個世紀，可是此埠居民的歷史記載，卻無人問津，這本書試行補此不足。

樂居埠居民乃排華時期最後的一批移民，他們如何設法辦到移民，本世紀初在加州的經歷、以及如何適應生活成為美國居民，均構成沙加緬度三角洲歷史重要的一環。三角洲農產豐裕，樂居埠居民功不可沒，而他們的歷史也極有趣味的。

一九七〇年華人人口二百五十人，至一九七六年減至六十四人，而至一九八〇年竟得四位。樂居埠是美國碩果僅存的農村華埠，可是該埠消失得甚速。近來非華人才開始在此居住。

十二人，第一代的有十八人，第二代十一人而第三代共十三人。

為求了解即將消失的樂居埠及居民，於一九七九年夏天，筆者和助手開始進行採訪，翌年夏天筆者個人繼續訪問，共探訪了廿個居民，都年過六十五歲且長居於斯，其中二人是婦人，其他十八人均是男人。除了一人外，所有均生於中國，訪問都用廣東話進行的。

一九八一年夏天，筆者再進行訪問，以便澄清及獲取更多資料，一些在樂居埠以外居住的，例如居於葛庯、汪古魯及沙加緬度的，都進行訪問，除了華人外，更訪問了有關的美國農人，美籍華農，一些商人及其他長居於三角洲而知道早期歷史的。全部共訪問了約五十人，每人的訪問約二小時至十五小時不等，有些人只訪問過一次，有些則達五次甚至十次之多。口述史料的搜集並不容易，有些不願提過去的事，甚者更表示疑心及不信任的，尤其每當問及他們早年的情況，此種心態屢見不鮮。

鳴　謝

在一九八〇年期間，樂居鎮不但成了一個受人矚目和關注的目標，亦成爲主張「開發」及「環保」兩派人仕的爭奪戰場，雙方揭起一場場的辯論，爭取社會各方面的支持。樂居鎮在春夏季節的週末裡，旅遊巴士穿梭不絕；電視台也曾在此探訪和拍攝紀錄片；學者、學生亦以該鎮爲題撰寫文章與論文；加州立法議會、公園管理局及房屋重建局亦公開聽取各方意見並鄭重討論研究如何保存樂居鎮的方案。

爲了保持客觀的意見，筆者在這期間避開各方面的爭論而專心於搜集這批華工的生活資料。

無論將來「環保」或「開發」獲勝，紀錄樂居鎮華工的歷史資料是極有意義的工作。

出版英文初版的工作曾蒙各方的支持，英文初版主編由馬女士主持，又經史篤先生、亞泰先生、馬先生組成編輯委員會審核，發此書的技術問題亦獲戈力格教授及賀女士的處理。後來更獲許多讀者朋友的捐款和預購，終於克服了出書的種種問題，筆者在此向各位致謝。

加州州務卿余江月桂來函說：

「『田園生涯』一書紀錄了早期華工在美國農田上苦苦爭扎的血汗史實，更把他們的社會及經濟生活紀錄下來，留傳後世。我認爲此書對於了解華人在早期加州農業上所扮演的角色有着重大的貢獻。加州議員若翰格蘭孟帝說：記載中國移民在加州三角州的文獻極爲缺乏及難尋，但這些中國農民對這三角州業發展的貢獻是不容忽視的。該書正好爲歷史文獻補充了這許多遺漏了的記錄。無論是中國人或是非中國人都能了解到辛勞的中國移民爲開發加州所扮演過非常重要的角色，另外本人亦感謝筆者爲三角州豐富的種族文化結構補上了新的一頁。

英文版問世後，筆者獲得學術界和對歷史有興趣的社團邀請講學。在此期間，筆者又將收集了的圖片加以整理，並編成了一套大型的展覽，亦被安排展出十餘次之多，筆者覺得雖然各方面的工作都能完成了，但還是有一心願未能達成，就是搜集資料期間，那些農工誠懇要求筆者出版中文版，使不諳英語的華人亦能認識這三角州的華人生涯是怎樣的一回事。

得蒙在港的三十年好友、中學和大學的舊同學賴俊傑先生於教學外不辭勞苦、答允協助將英文本翻譯成中文，花了兩年時光終於做好譯稿。後來又蒙海外華僑通訊社楊建成博士秉力支持，書稿於一九九二年榮獲臺灣財團法人海華文教基金會的出版獎助金，在楊博士的協助策劃下，不但中文版能出版，更難能可貴的是英文第二版亦同時一起出版，筆者對學長賴俊傑先生及楊建成博士的大力支持銘感於心。該書代表筆者從事教學工作廿多年最值得慶幸的一件大事。本人除感謝梁賀山先生的封面設計，加大戴維斯大學亞美學系和內子張愛齡多方的協助外，亦將此書獻給加州沙加緬度三角州的華人農工，紀念他們對加州農業發展的莫大貢獻。

鳴　謝

寫於加州戴維斯大學　一九九三年春

梁靜源

五

導　言

沙加緬度三角洲是加尼福尼亞州奇境之一，超過七百五十方哩的一群人工建造的島嶼和一千五百多哩的水域都是風景勝地。早期，數以千計的苗禾族的印第安人曾居住於三角洲的沼澤地帶，十八世紀時，西班牙傳教士和拓荒者開始在加州定居，一八二七年後，美國白人至此居住並在三角洲上種麥牧牛。加州併入美國版圖後不久，一八四八年哥羅馬（Coloma）金礦的發現，使三角洲成為往金礦上丘的通路，礦工可由此沿著沙加緬度河及聖祖昆河而抵達礦區。

一八五〇年代，人們多認為三角洲深具農業發展潛力，這一帶泛濫頻繁的沼澤地正展開墾殖，州議會於一八六一年通過防止河水泛濫法案，鼓勵築河堤。築堤極為艱苦，要常在水深齊腰中工作，瘧疾仍在當地流行。華工們建排水溝，造防洪水閘，堆疊河堤，在此情況下，於一八六〇年至一八八〇年間，開墾了八千八百畝地。河堤日後雖用先進設備重建，這些華工所築河堤卻奠下今日河堤網及三角洲農業的基礎。

自從三角洲適於農耕後，華工留下耕耘，一八七〇年代，千餘位華工成為農工或佃農。

一八八二年美國制定排華法案及其他立法以防止華工入境，三角洲華工人口便開始下降，一九二〇年代及一九三零年代雖稍有增加，但自二次大戰以來，人口穩定地減少，直至今日人數不足十人的華農仍留於三角洲耕耘。然而，華工使肥沃土壤成爲主要農業區並經而確定加州農產品之世界領導地位。

三角洲除了是農業要地外，還是風光優美之境。三角灣環境，到處均可提供林林種種的戶外活動，不論是划船、野營、觀鳥、釣魚、郊遊或是瀏覽各種奇趣小鎮，都使人賞心悅目。釣魚和划船是最普遍而受人喜愛，各種魚類如魚斑鱸（Catfish，striped bass）、鱘魚、鮭魚及鋼頭魚（Steel head）等都可獲得，沙灘、船塢及其他各種水上設施均不計其數，難怪每年都有數百萬人從加州四面八方湧到此地享用各種設施。

沙加緬度三角洲的歷史古跡和風景名勝著實不少。一六〇高速公路沿著蜿蜒曲折的沙加緬度河岸，出了沙加緬度便是具有一百廿年的菲蔔（Freeporr）小鎮，這個東倒西歪的市鎮並不在城市發展之列，隨後的萬頃田莊已蓋上了住宅和商業樓宇，當地農人（他們的先人早在一八八〇年代便在此墾殖）自然不樂於接受現代發展。

沿著一六〇公路，胡德（Hood）是第二個城鎮，建立於一九〇九年，以南太平洋鐵路總工程師威廉胡德（Wm．Hood）命名，該鎮人口約五百人。在一片的梨園中，建有豪華的維多利亞式之農場主人住宅，由一世紀前的拓荒者所建，宏偉壯觀。此外，昔日農工所居的眾多棚屋雖已坍倒，仍舊可見陳跡。

一六〇公路之右是沙加緬度河，之左是遍地田野，交替種植梨樹和穀物。冬天，沿路可見三兩農工站在梯頂修剪梨樹，有時更可見到由樹木薰蒸而生的一縷淡黃色薰煙從梨林中升起。冬季的梨樹均告光禿無葉，有些修剪得如巧奪天工，有些仍是亂枝橫生，等待著修枝者的剪裁。每當春天，燦爛的萬里梨花漫向天空，展顏而笑，招蜂惹蝶。田上又開始披上青裝，在夏間，纍纍的梨子掛在萬綠叢中，田野上遍地的玉米和菜蔬正同遍野的梨樹爭妍鬥麗。

每年七月份，一年一度的梨子節日在葛倫舉行，葛崙則在胡德鎮的下游。三角洲是美國重要產梨區，佔加州產量百分之卅，也是全美最早植梨地帶，佔地六千畝，平均每年產量達十萬噸。三角洲之產量平均每畝產梨十三至十四噸而全國之平均產量是每畝九至十噸。

葛崙的梨節在一所中學操場舉行，這個小鎮致力於此節日，要籌劃經年，這一天的節日，音樂表演、各種不同的梨子展覽、剝梨比賽、巨梨鬥重、梨果包裝示範和梨果入罐比賽等是為整天節日的特色。

在離開葛崙前，遊人會給舊葛崙銀行大樓的美色所迷，這幢美觀的建築物建於一九二〇年，在三角洲各鎮中最為堂皇壯嚴；而且，葛崙銀行更是推進三角洲農業開發重要因素之一。

過了葛崙，沙加緬度河再受人垂注，高速滑水艇在河上泛起白浪片片，豪華遊艇滿載遊人在河上往來不息而遊客卻可欣賞三角洲的祥和優美景色。在昔日，沙加緬度河曾是重要航道，連接三藩市灣和加州中心，一八六〇年代，輪船如加蘇比力號（Chrysoplis）、內華達號（Neveda）、柔仙美的號（Yesemite）、華施號（Washoe）和首都號（Capitol）均是基本河運交通工具，不幸的是這些輪船常因鍋爆裂引起災禍，例如一八六五年十月十二日，柔仙美的號（Yesemite）則自里傲威士打（Rio Vista）啓航便著火，船身在爆炸中猛沖上天再散跌入河中和碼頭上，約八十乘客死亡，船上所有華人無一倖免。

輪船雖常遭意外，但仍要沿河載運旅客和水果，由沙加緬度至三藩市及沿河各鎮。在三角洲的農業發展上，輪船曾扮演重要角色，其中以皇帝號和皇后號最大、最豪華及最著名。這兩艘船，部份在蘇格蘭建造而於一九二六年在加州市作頓（Stockton）完成，它們均長二百八十五呎，重一千八百卅七噸，置有二千磅重機器，可載二百卅八名乘客和二千噸貨物。這兩艘輪船於黃昏六時在三藩市開航而翌晨五時半抵達沙加緬度，在一九二〇年代，來回船票價值一元五角；於一九四一年停止服務。

葛崙後之另一小鎮是樂居鎮（Locke），一個可能只有七十人的小埠，是北美洲最後的一個農村華埠，也是本書焦點所在地。古舊屋宇和街道，稀少華人和獨特的歷史，都是以令人留連於此，登上週末觀光車，車上觀光客恐比鎮上居民還多之虞。橫過樂居沼地便是汪古魯鎮，它和其他沿河市鎮一樣，鎮上只有五至六家酒樓，數百居民和小撮華人和日本人，鎮後一片果園，鎮前是一座大的鐵吊橋，一六○公路通過此橋沿著河堤再走十多哩，即抵達三角洲最後的一個小鎮里奧威士打（Rio Vista），該鎮位於兩大幹線之交匯點，其一通往加州中央山谷，另一往三藩市灣地區而出了三角洲地帶，重返文明之地。

三角洲的浪漫風光及所具之生產力，一方面在於河水得以控制，另一方面有賴於農工辛勞，而兩者均和築堤及墾殖的華工有關。曾經人數眾多的華工，而今只能偶然一見；一度繁盛的華埠和華工村落，至今幾乎消萎無蹤，然而，先輩留傳下來的仍在。為了追尋過往，獨自跑到三角洲僅餘的樂居華埠，憑著鎮上和其他地方人士所見所聞，試行重編三角洲上的華人歷史，並且使北美洲僅存的華人鄉村免於湮沒無聞。

第一輯 樂居埠和加州沙加緬度三角洲的華工

第一章 華人移民的歷史

從中國古籍報導，皇帝的航海探究員最早曾於第五世紀在美西岸登陸，可是近代華人在加州的歷史卻自十九世紀中葉開始。有人指出有少量華人於一八四八或四九年由秘魯抵達加州（秘魯意圖使他們成爲奴隸），也有人認爲華人最早到加州是在一八四八年二月二日，由查理基利卑（Charles V. Gillespie）乘「鷹號」的雙桅船在三藩市泊岸，從中國帶來了二男一女，男的成爲礦工而女的成爲他的女僕。三藩市之星報（San Francisco Star）一八四八年四月一日刊載的一篇文章曾說及兩三華人在市中出現，而官方資料指出那時大約有五十華人已在加州。

一八四八年在失打保（Sutter's Mill）發現金礦的消息傳到三藩市後，尋金熱從此展開，與此同時湧現的便是華人的移民潮，和其他人一樣都住在金礦區奔竄。以一八五一年爲例，進入加州的華人達二千七百一十九人（而在一八二〇年至一八五〇年間，總數也不過一百人）。

在一八五〇至五一年湧進加州的華人均移自廣東南部沿岸一帶，且爲未婚的男子，他們多作暫時逗留，希望在短期間淘金致富而榮歸故里的，他們出自貧窮之家，在家鄉無蚨爲生，除了耕地不足，了無生計的地理和社會因素外，政治的原因都觸發他們遠涉重洋的打算。

十九世紀中葉，滿清皇朝的閉關政策嚴禁移民，對移居他國而返國者施以斬首刑罰，中國傳統觀念及社會和宗教都不鼓勵遠遊，朝野視西方爲未開化者，不主張和外國通商，在一八四〇年之前，全國只開放廣東省的廣州對外通商；因此，廣州地區人民由於接觸外商較多而最爲了解歐美情況，當加州金礦發現的消息傳到，遂引起人們尋金念頭。

促使華人到加州的近因不僅由於尋金的原因，種種天災人禍也是主因，從一八四〇至一八七〇年，中國發生一連串的災禍，較嚴重的如週期性的水災和旱災及引致的大荒與及人口過多等，不但使舉國貧困，且成爲動亂之根源，最後也使滿清於一九一一年滅亡。

政治禍亂使滿清沒落，而相繼的統治者均腐敗無能，無從使國家富強，一八四二年鴉片戰爭敗於英國，一八五六年英法聯軍戰役亦戰敗，結果使更多地方被逼迫對外開放，鴉片偷運更普遍，外國商品使固有工業萎縮不振，白銀不斷外流造成通貨膨脹（中國當時以白銀為本位），因對英法用兵而加重賦稅，使佃農更形窮困。遂引致太平天國於一八五一年起義對抗清朝，這期間的廣東珠江三角洲一帶，不少叛變和起義，民間動亂不息，田園變成廢墟，難以生息，於是移居〝金山〞似可作一理想出路。

即使不少人願往加州，卻甚少人能付得起旅費，有些人可從家人籌錢支付，其他則向一些移民機構舉債，以在美工作相當月份或年份的工資作為償還，太平洋中央鐵路公司（Central Pacific Railroad）藉這些機構開始於一八六六年僱用華工，在加州建造鐵路。

第一次華人移民潮湧往尋金，但金礦生產於一八五〇年代中期已告下降。第二次的移民浪潮卻由太平洋中央鐵路公司所容納，當時的白人、墨西哥人、印第安人或其他的勞工均不足，遂大量僱用華人建造橫越大陸的西段鐵道。這些華工縱使有語言隔膜，仍以勤勞及肯學而著稱。鐵路在一八六九年完工，在尋金式微及鐵道完成後，加州人口分佈的統計已由山區轉變為市鎮及農地，經濟活動也由採礦和築路轉為製造業和農業。

在三藩市，失業的鐵路工人從事洗衣業、製衣業、雪茄製煙業、造鞋業和經營餐館等，那些定居於蘇努馬（Sonoma）和拿巴（Napa）區的均有助於葡萄園的發展，而在橙縣

（Orange）區南部，華人的農業知識對種植廣袤的橙樹是不可或缺，定居於沙加緬度河三角洲的都受僱於土地開墾及農務。

沙加緬度河和聖祖昆河的匯合點是一片肥沃土地，這一帶沿地形成一連串的沙洲，直至十九世紀中期，每年泛濫都使這一帶土地不能用作農田。據說呂賓郭車勞（Reuben Kerchva）是第一位築堤壩者，他於一八五二年在格蘭島（Grand Island）上築河堤防止沙加緬度河水泛濫，由於騾馬不宜在柔滑泥炭上載運建築物料，他遂僱用華人、格拿加族（Kanakas）和印第安人。第一道河堤陸續給洪水毀壞，及至一八七〇年代，築堤技術有所改進，土地開墾得以進展，而華工在建造這些新堤上是不可缺的人力。

當所墾土地終於適於農業，華工留下種植、耕耘、和收割所宜生長的農作物。大部份研究都顯示以穀物為最早的主要農作物，直至一八七〇年代中期，果類及菜蔬種植的經濟價值更見顯明，罐頭工廠也於果園和農田旁興起以便處理所收穫的農產品。

華工既勤勞且工作效率高，又能迅速學習每種新職，大體上他們均非遊手好閒或只顧享樂，他們來美目的可作最好的解釋：大部份都希望在加州賺取足夠金錢回歸中國故鄉，置田買屋以安享晚年；部份華工如願以償，但絕大部份卻不能只作短暫過客而要終生營役。他們把大部份所得寄回祖家供養雙親妻兒乃至叔伯兄弟姊妹及其他家人，華工節衣縮食，所餘下的少許金錢僅可糊口及聊供消遣之用。多數華工均無意在美長期定居，亦無操流利英語的需要，也不接納美洲風俗，彼此結伴只在消除孤獨和寂寞，保存中國習俗以維繫思鄉情懷。

雖然華工們不作長居之想，他們對加州和外國風俗仍感興趣，少數華工學習英語，充作同胞的傳譯員，有些接受西服而美國化，有一定數目的華工仍願積極參與所生活的新天地，從而肯定自己的價值。

華人的友善獲當地美國人的回報，在三藩市舉行的美國第十二任的泰勒總統（Zachery Taylor）喪禮，華人被邀請為主禮之一，在其他慶典或節日，華人均有參與協助。在鐵道陣營中，華人也被重視，即使其他礦工對華工仍感生疏，但最初並沒把華人逐出礦區，而華工通常在那些曾被白種尋金者所棄置的礦區上採礦。這種容忍華工採礦的態度並不長久，當一八五〇年代中期的金礦產量開始減少時，美國礦工聯同北歐人對外來的黑人包括華人感到憤怨，設法使加州保留給白人。

隨著的廿年中，白人對有色人種的憤懣轉為故意。南北戰爭對東部工業的影響結果，即使加州新創的初期工業可與之匹敵，加州就業機會因而提高，由於勞工短缺，工資可說高於全國，但南北戰爭末期，更重要的是大陸鐵路通車之後，情況急劇改變，東部工業復甦，逼使太平洋沿岸的公司面臨破產的威脅。鐵路每日載來更多的投機者到此「日照之地」圖利，於是形成過量的非熟練工人，當一八六〇年代晚期，經濟衰退打擊東部，並於一八七〇年代初期禍及加州，衆矢之的之廉價華工即首當其衝，成爲代罪羔羊。

在各種法案上，加州力圖排除「黃禍」，一八五五年的外國礦工稅主要是向墨西哥人和華人征收，同年的華人乘客稅在乎把華人趕出美國，接踵而來的有一八五八年州立排外法案，一八六二年保障白人勞工法案及其他的種族歧視立法等。雖然這些法例大都由最高法院宣佈不合乎憲法，但加州的排華已是根深蒂固，而且內戰之後，聯邦政府爲了開拓新局面，也在渴望能安撫加州。

一八六六年卜零根（Burlingame）條約，中美間訂立了關於移民及其他事務的互惠權益，可是一八八〇年的條約修訂卻只由美國單獨決定移民限額，而排華條例及一八八二年的法例把大部份新的華人移民暫停十年並且否定華人入籍之公民權，一八八八年的司各脫（Scott）法案更進一步限制華人移民，並使居住在美國華人離美後更難返美。一八九二年吉釐（Geary）法案延長排華十年並於一九〇二年排華法案成爲永久性，這些法案維持至一九四三年都沒有廢止（一九四三年華人重獲公民權），就是一九四三年後，只有絕少華人可獲入境，直至一九六五年，華人移民才和其他各國移民一樣列於同等地位。

種族歧視法案並不足以滿足反華情緒，以丹尼堅尼（Denis Kearney）勞工團體爲首，一八六〇年代，華人乘船登岸均集中於三藩市船塢，飽受白人暴徒的嘲弄甚至用石頭投擲，在礦營裏發生不少暴力事件，小鎮中的中國城（華埠）遭人放火，居民給槍逐出鎮外，遠至洛杉機、懷俄明州的石泉事件（Rock Spring Wyoming），每次騷動都有大量華人給白人所殺，這些暴行和歧視法例使華人移民數字自一八六〇至七〇年間的十二萬三千人，於卅年間跌至一萬五千人。一九〇〇年後，數字下降更顯著，直至一九六五年，甘廼迪總統取消移民限額，華人移民都為數極少。

排華法案用意旨在防止華工入境，但教師、學生、商人和遊客仍准入境，在美居住之華商妻子及土生華人的妻子均可獲准進入美國。此外，排華法案仍有漏洞可尋，不少設法證明是商人而獲入境，另外有一種「冒籍入境法」流行起來，一名土生華人可返回中國一個時期娶妻生子，返美國後向政府申報在中國已生了個孩子，即使沒有孩子又或生的是個女孩子，都申報一個兒子，當局發給他一張出生紙作為他日申請入境之證明，十五或廿年後，這張出生紙可以賣給在中國的家人或其他年青人，假稱是出生紙所證明的兒子亦稱「買紙仔」得以入境，這種「買紙仔」售價雖昂貴，仍有人極願嘗試赴美謀生，在嚴厲排華期間，很多是透過這種冒籍入境方法而入境。一九〇六年三藩市地震和大火毀去了所有移民紀錄，美國官員難以決定是原籍或冒籍孩子，更有助於此種冒籍方法通行。

一九一〇年至一九四〇年間，美國在三藩市灣的天使島上設立拘留所，審查所有入境華人，男女分隔在不同房間裡，其他移民可以迅速過境，但華人移民卻在此往往住上數星期甚至數月，證件被查了又查，一次再次地問話，遭受恐嚇和羞辱，這種可怕的遭遇，使許多移民終生難忘。此島最後在一九四〇年由於環境污垢不宜居住而關閉。

在沙加緬度三角洲上的華人，最常見的移民方法不是以合法妻兒身份便是以「買紙仔」身份入境，他們都是同一族人或鄉人聚居一處，三角洲上聚居的華人以來自四邑和中山為主，四邑人和中山人彼此亦有互相仇視，即使到了美國亦然。樂居埠也是中山埠，下章即在

說及廣東中山縣。

第二章 在華南中山縣的故鄉

位於中國東南部的廣東是沿岸一個重要省份，省會廣州居於南部珠江口，距中國南海僅八十浬，全省面積方圓九萬二百四十七平方哩，人口達四千二百八十萬。北部地區多山，人口較少。南部擁有人口稠密及地勢平坦的珠江三角洲。由於地近赤道，氣候溫暖，全年平均溫度為華氏七十二度。夏季延續七至八個月。溫暖氣候，豐足雨量及肥沃土壤，促使廣東省原（廣東南沿岸地區）。由於種植季節長，每年可收成多次。

（尤其是珠江三角洲）成為農產區，耕地佔全省面積百分廿而大部份在珠江三角洲及潮汕平

珠江是廣東最大河流，匯合東江、西江和北江。三角洲佔地相當於全省百分之五面積，和夏威夷島相若，即使如此，其產量卻佔全省農量的一半，物產以甘蔗、稻、薯、桑（桑供果園及魚塘之用）為主。三角洲在地形上較特別，有平地和山丘，這些山丘本為海灣中之小島，河流之淤沙充塞河口，使小島和陸地連接，這種淤塞仍繼續往其他海島沖積。三角洲土地大都用作耕地，其他均用作城鎮、農村、魚村及工業用地。大部份工業均為農作物加工、

二一

織絲、提煉蔗糖、製造農田化學品及建築材料。三角洲水道縱橫，成為廣東省水運中心，運輸水果、蔗糖、甘蔗、牛類、魚類、食鹽、木材及布料等。

過去數百年來，珠江三角洲都劃分七個縣，中山縣最為富庶。一個連接海灣的丘陵地帶，原稱香山，因這帶經常盛開大量花朵所生的芳香而得名，馥郁的花香，據說在十里外都可覺察。一九二五年改名中山，紀念革命之父孫逸仙先生（中山為國父別字之一，他生於香山縣）。

方圓一千卅方哩之中山縣可分三個不同地理環境地區，中部多丘陵，北部為平地，南部沿岸地區多島嶼。平地河道繁多，緊扼灌溉及水運。沿著河道，內地和海岸相通。處於廣州市和數個大城市之要衝，接近比廣州更近的葡屬澳門及自由港的香港，是為廣東省及中山縣通往非華人社會及國際市場之窗。

廣州市

位於珠江口的古舊廣州，不但是華南最大城市且是廣東省會。歷代都為重要通商口岸。十六世紀及十七世紀，西方人開始經常來往廣州。一六八四年英國東印度公司在此設立代辦並壟斷國際貿易而至一八三四年。由一七五七年至一八四〇年，廣州是為對外通商唯一合法之地，出口以絲綢、茶葉及瓷器爲大宗，進口主要有鴉片、棉花和紡織品。大概在一八四○年後，入口遠超出口。

廣州是個美麗迷人的城市，包括市郊在內，共有一百廿五所寺廟，五層的高塔及天主教堂的尖頂高入雲霄。該市的古董、青銅器、象牙雕刻、刺繡、銀器、酸枝傢俱、屏風、瓷器及玉雕，聞名遐爾。人口稠密，一九七五年，廣州人口超過三百萬。週圍地區雖是農產豐富，糧食仍不能自給，需要進口。

對外通商的重要影響便是鼓勵居民移民海外，中國海外移民有半數以上是來自廣州及附近地域。大部份移民海外的都是貧困者，希望賺取金錢帶回家鄉。在十七至廿世紀期間，不惜以各種非法途徑移民海外，多湧往東南亞、北美洲及其他海外地方。

香港

香港距廣州九十里，距澳門四十里，爲英國殖民地，世界重要貿易和國際中心。面積四百平方里，包括香港島、九龍半島及新界和二百卅六個大小島嶼，均散佈在珠江口一帶。一百五十年前，英國人到此之前，香港只是一個小漁村，鴉片戰爭後，清朝於一八三八年割港島及九龍予英國，爲英國最後一個殖民地，在一八三八至九八年間，再租新界給英廷，爲期九十九年而於一九九七年期滿交回中國。香港前途將告不穩定，有格外於中英雙方的談判。

（註：中英政府於一九八四年簽署協議，同意香港主權於一九九七年屬於中國並保持香港政制五十年不變，即使如此，民心仍不安定。）

十九世紀後半期及廿世紀早期，香港發展為重要國際商港，人口由一八五一年的三萬三千人增至一九五〇年的二百五十萬而達今日超過五百萬。人口急升主要由於大量難民流入，難民源自中國的天災人禍，今日大部份香港居民都由於逃避中國共黨的統治。迅速增長的人口與及一九四九至五二年間流入難民多為工業人才，近數十年間使香港展開工業革命，吸引外資和外國企業及大量遊客，自一九六〇年以來，香港逐漸成為世界第三金融中心，僅次於紐約和倫敦。

澳門

澳門和羅馬一樣建於七個山丘上，位於中國南部海岸，於一五五七年葡人探勘中所發現。面積僅只六平方里的半島，北部緊接中國，是通往中山縣的門戶。

十七世紀，澳門成為商人和傳教士往來中國和日本的要地。澳門的繁盛和優越地位，使其他西歐國家也對之唾涎而密謀攫取。當中國沿岸商港開放通商，及一八四一年英人在香港殖民後，澳門的經濟地位開始下降；可是，澳門仍繼續作爲輸出魚米布匹和其他中國物產的重要港口。澳門深受葡萄牙的影響，古典伊伯利亞式的教堂，散佈著大砲的城堡，用石卵鋪成的蜿蜒街道，與及古老建築物和紀念碑等都可見一斑；不過，澳門始終仍是華人城市，華人佔人口二十六萬一千人。

中山縣

珠江流經中山縣東南部，近河一帶均是沙地，有稻田、桑田和魚塘，桑樹、蠶絲和魚塘互相支援而成一整體工業，桑業養蠶，樹根鞏固沙土使低地成爲魚塘，蠶糞餵魚而魚糞作爲桑樹肥料，這是中山縣農業的生態循環現象，其他物產尚有香蕉和荔枝。

一九二〇年左右，中山縣人口約八萬七千人，土壤肥沃，每年產米超過人口所需，而且中山縣供應鄰近鄉縣大部份的糧食，甚至供應廣州，和各鄰縣比較，中山最爲富庶。即使如此，仍有不少人移民海外謀生或求學。容閎是第一位留學美國的中國學生，在一八五四年畢業於耶魯大學。周崧（Joe Shoong）乃一位成功商人，於一九二〇年代在加州設立一元商店（National Dollar Stores），他們均是中山人。

然而，大部份中山移民並不富有，或顯赫有名又或受過良好教育，在樂居埠的中山居民大都是沙加緬度三角洲的農工或佃農，他們來美前在華的情況均較爲顛沛，樂居埠一位老居民吳壽容說道：

「我生於中國中山縣的東村，十多歲時，在叔伯的果園工作，那裡種植多種水果，例如桃、李子、荔枝、枇杷和紅橘。那時在中國難以謀生，糧食不足，到處失業，而我整天做農工的工錢只有一角錢，但我已算幸運，獲得親戚的僱用。由於貧困，很多人決定離鄉別井往外國謀生，勝於在家鄉捱苦。」

鄭保在一九一八年到美定居於樂居埠，他憶述：「我生於中山濠頭村，從十歲至十二歲入學了兩年，以做散工爲生，最初爲一間店舖往各農家收集雞蛋以便運往香港，後來轉做人力車伕，接載往來鄉村和城鎮的人客，這種工作十分辛苦且需要很大氣力，但那時還年青，我並沒幹多久便想轉行，在一九一八年，從親友等籌借一筆錢便決定來到美國。」

何蘭淸也補充說：「在中國時，當我還未結婚前，祖母不容許女子上學的，她認爲女子求學沒有用處，所以我只懂做飯和在田裡工作。因爲中日戰爭爆發，我在一九三〇年代來到美國；那時候，我的丈夫是三角洲上的一個農夫。」

第三章　沙加緬度三角洲的華埠

沙加緬度三角洲是沙加緬度河和聖祖昆河間一帶的肥沃低地，從安迪昂，提里斯，市作頓（Antioch，Tracy，Stockton）和沙加緬度劃一直線，在這界限範圍內是爲三角洲，是加州重要農業區之一，而農業在加州居於第一位。整個三角洲都是農田、果園和大農場。大部份田地佔地廣闊，往往數百甚至數千畝。主要物產包括馬鈴薯、小麥、梨和番茄。除了田地外，三角洲上還有些小鎭，大都建立於一八五〇至六〇及七〇年代。

華人最早於一八六〇年代便抵達三角洲，多來自珠江三角洲的四邑和中山，而以來自中山的爲數最多，他們多從事營商、理髮、洗衣、餐館及包工等，絕大多數均爲農工或佃農，而早期（一八六〇年和一八七〇年代）則爲築堤工人。

築堤是爲了開墾三角洲肥沃土地作爲耕地，早期的築堤工作用人力；後來機器開始代替人力，用機械所築堤壩不但迅速且較堅固耐用。早年華工是人力的主幹，直至一八八〇年首宗排華法案才開始裁減華工。

華工既是最早成爲築堤開墾的勞工，但大批華工在一八六八年通過墾土議案，並堅決進行開墾時才抵達，那時正值第一條橫越大陸鐵道剛好完工，數以千計的華工遂自願轉往築堤，倖免於失業。

築鐵路華人的一貫工作制度亦用於築堤上，開發土地當局首先和一位懂英語的華工訂立合約，承建一定數量的河堤，這名華工是爲工頭及通譯員，他召集一幫華工並決定在何時何地工作以及作息時間，並且傳達僱主的命令，此外這幫華工通常有自己的伙伕，他們都住在工地的帳棚以免虛耗時間。每幫人數多少視乎工作大小而不同，有八人一幫也有卅人一群的。堤壩是用蘆葦泥磚築成平行的兩道角錐形牆，中間塞滿沙坭，有時用騾馬把堤頂弄平。這些華工所築堤壩都較小型且不能經受終年的河水滲透，只能作爲短暫的防洪。

築堤是一種辛苦費力的工作，爲了提高效果和省力，進行一些創新，華工首先設計一種蹄形狀比馬蹄較大，最初是用桫木板製造，穿上金屬絲綁在馬蹄作平場泥土之用。這種蹄把體重散佈於較大面積，而不易陷進軟泥裡；這樣，土地開墾較爲迅速和有效，由一八六○年至一八八○年，人工（主要是華工）所開墾的約建八千八百畝地。

華工的待遇低廉，最初的工錢，華人工頭承建合約是移掘一立方碼的河泥價錢爲一角三仙至一角三仙半，另一種工錢是支付工頭一元一天予每名工人，而工頭扣起一角或一角半，其餘的發給工人，至於僱用華工人數，從氾濫區墾土第三〇三號資料所記，由一八七七年七月一日至一八七八年十二月卅一日（共十八個月），總共支付華工款額達二十五萬三千七百八十元五仙，尚欠款項六千六百廿元八角四仙，佔此期總支出的百分七十二，可知最少有五百華工人數在築這段堤。

在艾德華和琳達、都拉（Dutra）於里奧威士打（Rio Vista）所經營的博物館，那裡有很多值得紀念的照片。古舊信件、會議紀錄簿、法律文件及人工製品，這些均記載三角洲挖泥歷史，其中有些文件提及華人築堤工人。都拉（Dutra）的父親是他家族中第一位僱用華工，據他所說，用人力在三角洲上墾土約有三千二百萬碼地，用挖泥機開墾土地則有九億一千三百萬。華工把挖起的泥鏟往手推著，再倒在駁船。他們並修築堤頂，而現在均可用機械代替。少數僅存的蘆葦鞋，也有一隻在博物館內陳列。

當地一位農夫柯利弗德‧斯密說：直至一九一八年仍有華工在築堤，他還記得他的父親是堤壩承建商，負責承建他們在格拉斯堡（Clarksburg）農場右前方的一段堤壩，他父親曾監督約八名華工。華工到河床鏟起沙礫泥垢，置於手推車裡，從而建起河堤。賓記起他母親曾提及他的祖父也有築堤，他母親說她所居住的葛崙常有泛濫，樂居埠的周厚起，人人都趕往搶修河堤。當泛濫警報響起，人人都趕往搶修河堤。

許多築堤工人都留在三角洲上當農工，很多住在三角洲上的小鎮，通常聚居於很小的華埠，同文同種及反華情緒逼使他們聚居於華埠。三角洲上最主要的華埠都在沙加緬度河沿岸，其中最顯著的五個華埠，依逆流而上之次序是爲理奧威士打，埃靈頓，汪古魯（Rio Vista、Isleton）、樂居埠及葛崙。

里奧威士打（Rio Vista）建立於一八五七年，初名白里素迪理奧（Brajos Del Rio），在一次洪水毀去後再於較高地面上重建。一八六二年改爲現名。於一八八〇年至一九二〇年代間，該鎮以世界最大蘆筍罐頭工廠而自豪，自一八七八年，鎮上前街北端開始建有華埠，約有六戶人家，那時候最傑出的是蔡周。美國華人公墓則座落於鎮外，其後屍體多已掘起而運回中國安葬。現今，公墓上只存有一名華人之墓，那是一九二七年逝世的一名婦女。

史超域特（Steward）先生的家族自一八九二年以來便在里奧威士打（Rio Vista）經營殯儀館，他記得一次華人奢華的葬禮，送殯行列買穿整個小鎮，送殯隊伍中有整隻燒豬和紙製肖像，例如紙屋是給死者鬼魂安息之所，還有樂隊伴著送殯行列往墓地。

一八九〇年代，里奧威士打（Rio Vista）提倡蘆筍爲經濟作物，擺脫不景的年代，而開始擴展地域和財富，華人亦分享此繁榮景象，農工和園工都有他們的假日，華人人口頗多，包括種植馬鈴薯的農夫和長期僱用的農工（大部份農工受僱於蘆筍農場），這些華工差不多來自四邑（尤其是台山）。一九一〇年至一九二〇年間，蘆筍田歉收，華埠首當其衝最先結束，現僅遺下早期華埠的一間房屋在鎮上，仍有少數華人在此居住和營商。

據一位學者所言，蘆筍發展爲經濟作物使三角洲上華人的都市化延遲了大約五十年，此影響整個三角洲，而以里奧威士打（Rio Vista）和埃靈頓（Isleton）爲最。埃靈頓（Isleton）由墨西哥戰爭時一位老兵名豪西亞浦（Josiah Pool）於一八七四年所建。人口調查報告指稱該鎮在一八八〇年有居民一千六百八十人，其中八百八十人是華人（佔百分五十二），其餘的是高加索人。以職業分類，華人多是農人或農工，只有少數是漁民、僕人和商人。在埃靈頓（Isleton）未建成前，華人早已開始向浦（Pool）先生租田耕種，他們種植甘薯、白豆及其他農作物，耕地約有四十四畝，農作物收成出售後，華人佃農付給浦（Pool）先生一千一百元。

埃靈頓（Isleton）是最早華人區，位於西南端鄰近洛扶陸區（Lothrop Tract）的積巨小河道（Jackson Slough）有居民三十五人，六至七戶人家，四間商店和一間洗衣店。華人區遭火燒毀了兩次，房屋都是木造而互相緊靠。一九一五年十二月的一次大火把全區夷爲平地。其後迅速重建，人口日多，可是又一次大火發生於一九二六年陣亡將士紀念日之後，把房屋都燒光了，於是再行重建。這次多用鐵皮頂、磚和石棉建造以便防火。除火災外，該鎮還有洪水之患，最近一次發生於一九七二年，由於河堤崩裂所致。目前仍有少量中國商人，他們自早期便已在此經商直至今天。

陳珠太太（Mrs. Gee Chin）於一九一一年在埃靈頓（Isleton）出生，生於斯而長於斯。她祖父在他的火柴廠（位於西艾納Sierras附近）給火燒毀後才到此鎮的，他告訴她那時候華人是用手製造火柴。他和夥伴在該鎮的舊華埠經營一間什貨店，這間店舖和其他相連的建築物都於一九二六年焚毀一空，後來他回中國退休，從此沒有回美。陳太太（Mrs Chin）的父親是在她少年時來美的，最初在西艾納（Sierras）的一間木廠做廚子，後來在父親經營的什貨店工作並經營一間餐館，一九二六年大火後，他在被燒毀了的店舖原址上重建，地點位於埃靈頓（Isleton）的主要街道。在一九二〇年代，華工除了在蘆筍田工作外，很多還在附近的馬鈴薯田裡工作，陳太太（Mrs. Chin）的父親供應糧食給這些種植馬鈴薯的農夫。她父親並沒有兒子，她是次女且最親近父親經常往店裡幫她父親料理店務，後來並承繼了這間店，現在該店稱爲埃靈頓釣魚用品店（Isleton Bait Shop），她大概會將該店留給她的孩子。在鎮上仍由華人擁有的還有兩間餐館（在埃靈頓釣魚用品店Isleton Bair Shop 的對面）和李氏運動用品店（Lee’s Sporting Goods）。

幼年的陳太太（Mrs. Chin），在一所男女分開的東方學校就讀，由第一班唸至第八班。

第一班的學生約十人而第八班時僅剩下四人（三名中國人一名日本人）。此外，她也到鎮上的華文學校唸中文，都是在下午及傍晚的時候上課，她說她很樂於學中文，這樣她可以和朋友說中文並可幫她父親記帳及售貨。

埃靈頓（Isleton）的華人只有中山和四邑人，彼此並沒有什麼問題，即使有爭吵的都和金錢有關，這些問題通常都由朋友協助下解決，又或到當地的社團秉公堂解決。陳太太（Mrs. Chin）的父親曾當了秉公堂的主席很多年。秉公堂的主要作用是保障鎮上華人的業務，其他主要活動便是聯絡和主辦一些集會，慶祝農曆新年及舉辦春茗。

一九二○年代至一九四○年代，是埃靈頓（Isleton）經濟最逢勃時期，除了華人，還有日本人和菲律賓人，都在華埠居住或常光顧華埠。除秉公堂及華人經營之商號外，華埠尚有四間賭館。陳太太（Mrs Chin）記得國民罐頭廠（National Cannery）是由一位華人名叫趙寬（Thomes Foon Chew）所購得，他從三藩市來此鎮，也是第二位華人獨自經營罐頭工廠，除了這間工廠外，其他罐頭廠都僱用很多華工，尤其是華婦更多。

在埃靈頓（Isleton）上游七里便是汪古魯鎮，此鎮由若翰拾柏（John W. Sharp）於一八五一年建立，那是一個十分細小的小埠，直至一八七○年代，來往三藩市和沙加緬度的汽船開始在此鎮停泊，橋頭或船橋也隨後建成。

華人大概在汪古魯鎮建立時便在足底居住，直至一九五〇年代，華人佔全鎮人口很大比例。早期的華人當是築堤工人而其他的不是果園工人便是農工，於一八八〇年代和一八九〇年代卻多是新開設的罐頭工廠工人，那時的華埠以餐館、雜貨店及其他商店最爲著名，其中有些店舖仍保留到今日。

直至二次大戰，汪古魯鎮和埃靈頓（Isleton）一樣，鎮上的華人隨著農業的週期而倏忽變動，有如埃靈頓（Isleton）一般，多數的華人都在果園或馬鈴薯農田工作。在汪古魯鎮，有很多華工宿舍由華人開設，於一九二〇年代，這些宿舍的租金平均是五元一個月租用一間房（兩張床）連同煮食地方。每當假日或雨天，農工便光顧華埠的賭館和妓寮，該鎮也有多間都在法例禁止之列。

汪古魯鎮的華埠遭受兩次大火焚毀，但每次火災後都重建，第一次發生於一九一五年，在此之前，鎮上華人都是四邑和中山人，均是珠江三角洲相鄰地區的同鄉，他們操不同方言且經常互相仇視，在中國如是，到了美國亦如是，這種敵對促使中山人在一九一五年大火後遷離該鎮，搬往樂居埠小鎮，樂居埠就在汪古魯鎮隔一條水道對岸。

汪古魯鎮華埠第二次大火發生於一九三七年，在第一次至第二次大火期間，由於葛崙鎮的華人湧入，華埠已恢復往日繁盛，一九三〇年葛崙埠遭火焚去，而那裡的地主不讓他們重建（那時的美國法例使華人不可能成為地主）。一九四〇年代後期，需要農工的人數大量下降，該鎮的華埠最後也告沒落。目前仍有少量仍在鎮上居住，三角洲上最成功的華人務農世家之一（方林彬之子）仍居在距離該鎮不到數里的地方。

黃有，一個已退休的農工，現居於樂居埠，他憶述當一九二一年初抵三角洲時，便和他父親居於汪古魯鎮，他們共住宿舍裡一間房，如開工便在田間用膳，不開工時便搜集一些柴枝在宿舍裡作燒飯之燃料。

馬林出生於中國，但在汪古魯鎮長大，並經營一間理髮店已有數十年了，他先在屋倫學習理髮，然後在三藩市工作了四個月，一九二九年時回到了汪古魯鎮，自己經營理髮店，當時鎮上共有八間理髮店，而他是唯一的華人理髮師。大概約八百華人在鎮上居住，在農忙時人口增加至一千人以上，整個鎮都擠著華人，他的理髮店和其他華人經營的生意都十分昌盛。他收的理髮費是五角，在最繁忙的日子，通常是週末，他一天工作超過十小時，每天可賺高達五十元。

馬林記得焚城的第二次大火，那是在一九三七年，在早上四時半起火，整整焚毀了八十間房屋，從公路到鐵路間整片地區，燒了四個小時才熄滅，他邊談邊向筆者指著很多從未重建仍舊空置的地段，有兩個退休的華人農工住在他店後的房屋便給燒死了，其中一位死時已超過六十歲。

一位現居於沙加緬度的鄭慶饒記起那個夏天，他在一間華人經營的什貨店工作，除了應付日常顧客外，他還負責在店裡收集彩票（類似白鴿票），買彩票的全是華工，那時很多華人商店在夏天都經售這種彩票作為副業，彩票由賭館經營而交店舖銷售，華人便不用往賭館購買了。

為了節制賭館業務及其他事務，也為了改善僱主和僱員間關係，秉公堂於一九一〇年代或一九二〇年代在汪古魯鎮設立分號，這個組織履行一些重要公衆活動：協助那些貧苦華人返回中國家鄉，運回死者的骸骨到其祖家下葬，每年主辦三個大節日的活動及宴會。在一九三〇年代、四〇年代及五〇年代且演出粵劇，它還有助於債務得以安全可靠，並且調解會員間的糾紛。簡言之，它是華埠一個最重要的社團組織。在一九三〇年代，尚有另一個華人慈善團體（中華會館），代表華人團體向美國當局說明或表達民意，而且曾經一個時期代替了秉公堂主辦一些社團活動，在一九四五年，這個社團組織卻消失了。

汪古魯鎮秉公堂的積極會員最頂點時達四百人，而埃靈頓（Isleton）甚至是葛崙的秉公堂卻因會員不足而關閉。最近逝世的孫博（Bob Suen），曾任多屆主席，據他說，近年來秉公堂的主要活動以一年的三大節日為重點（例如農曆新年、春茗），其次的社團活動例如舉辦高爾夫球賽等。它在社會的角色很有限，此由於其所管制的事務不多，也由於賭館生意不景氣以及三角洲上的華埠愈來愈萎縮的原故。

汪古魯鎮不到一里而位於水道對岸的是樂居埠，那是本書中心所在，將於下章述及，在此略去不提。在樂居埠十里外便是葛崙埠，是本書所提的三角洲上最後的一個古鎮。一位從礦工轉爲農人的占士先（James V. Sims）於一八六〇年代建立這個靜寂的小鎮，曾經因設立數間魚類罐頭廠而一度突趨繁榮，葛崙住著很多華人，華人聚居於此由於罐頭廠及周圍的果園，葛崙事實上是三角洲梨果的中心。

一九一〇年代和一九二〇年代，葛崙的華埠有五百華人而名噪一時，現在僅存一間店舖，這裡居住的有較長久居民、果園的園工和種植馬鈴薯的農工與及佃農，在一八七九年十二月當華埠焚毀時，一些華商計劃在鎮上開設製衣工廠，重建的民區即使經過兩次火災依然充滿活力，直至一九三〇年第四次火災才毀於一炬，這次地主不再續租約，大部份的居民遷往樂居埠和汪古魯鎮。

留在葛崙的華人再重建華埠的，其中主要人物是李應彬，是一位店主也是一個從一九〇八年居於汪古魯鎮的成功農人，他熱心社會公益且具生意頭腦，他大力協助一九三〇年火災後的重建，和前兩次火災後的重建情形一樣。在一九一〇年，他曾款待中國革命領袖孫逸仙先生，大力資助他推翻滿清，恢復中華，翌年一九一一年孫先生革命成功，成爲第一位臨時總統。後來再於一九三四年，李應彬和一些華人，促成汪古魯鎭中華會館的成立，此會館的建立爲了向中國抗日英雄蔡廷鍇將軍致敬，蔡將軍曾光臨葛崙埠。至一九四〇年代中期，李應彬一直都在每星期日，款待所有居住在鄰近地區的華人一頓雞飯的晚餐，據他兒子說，平均每次有四百農人和農工出席。

在較早時，於一九一五年，葛崙的華人創辦了一所華文學校，一九二〇年左右，華埠也設有秉公堂和中國國民黨支部，聲名大噪，華文學校直至一九四〇年才告結束，黨支部也在二次大戰結束後不久也告結束，秉公堂爲時較久，到而今也面臨滅亡的命運。今日葛崙的華埠差不多是李朵華（李應彬之子）所有，餘下的屬於一些美籍華工。

柯利弗德・斯密太太（她的丈夫往往爲了馬鈴薯而嚴責華人農工）憶起一些事，當她年靑時，她的家在葛崙華埠附近，一個年老的華婦常帶她的孫女到葛崙上學，有一天，她的狗咬了這老婦的孫女，老婦到她家討了一束狗毛，後來知道這位老婦把狗毛和一些中藥搗成糊狀，包在她孫女給狗咬的傷口，那個小孫痊癒了，這個小孫仍活著，住在三藩市，現在已有七十歲。斯密夫人仍記得她的一個華人女同學，這個女同學在幼年時便學習駕駛飛機，這種勇氣使她印象深刻。

除了上述故事外，很少提及三角洲上華人的妻子和女兒，前章曾指出美國對移民的限制，使華人難以攜同他們的妻子到美國。異族通婚法例和中國習俗均限制華人和異族通婚，商人不在移民限制之列，很多商人帶同他們的妻子，但對一般農工和佃農，這是不可能的事（為此，華埠妓寮也隨之旺盛起來）。

普通的華工，成家立室唯一可行的方法是返中國結婚，可是也並不容易，往往因金錢不足而延遲。一位樂居埠退休的農工說他在廿一歲離開中國，他返中國結婚時已三十五歲。接受訪問的一位佃農，他十二歲便來美，他在一九二〇年回中國探他母親一次，但要等到一九二七年二次返華時才有足夠經濟能力結婚，換言之，他要花去十五年的光景才有點經濟基礎，有些華工永遠沒法返華討老婆，原因之一是金錢不足，那是由於耽於賭博，賭博確是一種很大的誘惑，一位單身的農工訴說他當時沒有其他任何娛樂，身邊也沒有親人可以管束他，假如他的朋友對他說聲一起去賭錢的話，他便和他一道去了，賭博令人興奮不已，如果賭輸了，便再工作，這樣那能積蓄金錢呢！

當一個人在美國辛勞地工作了多年而返回故鄉探望家人親友，那是多麼令人欣喜若狂，倘若他要回鄉娶親，他的家人便會安排一切，給他物色妻子，打點婚事的一切大小事宜，商議嫁妝，訂定婚宴等，當他抵達家鄉後，婚事即可進行，他要支付一切的費用，也因此會耗盡他辛苦所賺的收入。一位農工黃有確認他在一九三五年回鄉結親，曾花去了三千元，包括旅費、新娘的嫁妝、男女雙方家人的喜酒及所有親朋乃至全村的酒席。他還買了一所房子和幾畝田以便他的妻子生活有所保障。婚後不久，丈夫便要返回美國謀生，而美國政府只准許他離開美國十至十二個月。孩子通常在他父親回美國後才出生。如果一對夫婦沒有孩子，便領養一個兒子，姑不論怎樣，做父親的往往並不認識在家鄉由母親撫養的孩子。

農工孫社才說道：「我回鄉結婚，我的大女在一九二二年出世時我已回到美國了。」他的長女陳太著說：「我記得在年青時見過父親好幾次，我知道他是父親但對他的一切都不知道，我不知道他在美的工作，只覺得他對家庭很好，寄錢回來養家。」

黃有的兒子說：「在我移民到美國前的日子裡，我記起只見過父親一次。我知道我有父親，因為母親常在講他，同時常常收到寄來的信和金錢，當我們終於住在一起時，我們互相之間竟不能溝通。」

很多華工在家鄉都有家室，並且忠於自己的家，然而在美國卻享受不到家庭生活，他們只是在養活那遠在另一世界的家而已。

至於那些非法進入美國的華工，他們不可能離開美國，即使他們有足夠金錢也談不上回鄉娶妻。他們直至一九五〇年代時，他們移民身份得以修正後，終於可以回鄉結婚，而他們也已屆五十或六十歲了。他們回香港找個年輕妻子，仍可娶得妻子，一方面由於他們有錢，另一方面香港在一九五〇年代有大量難民從中國大陸跑到香港，在香港生活困難，所以也有女子願意嫁給老人的，這種婚姻多由親戚安排，希望她嫁到美國後，將來家人有機會也可以移往美國。

第四章 加州的樂居埠

樂居埠並非在加州所建立的第一個華埠，也非三角洲上唯一的華埠，然而它是僅有的一個農村華埠能持續至今，並且足可象徵華人經歷重要的一面，和對該州所作的貢獻。儘管它的特性曾數度更迭，卻始終和三角洲的農業繫結在一起。

樂居埠是由一所宿舍、一間賭館和一片酒吧而起的，都是由三位華人小商人於一九一二年所創設的，而設立的理由基於南太平洋鐵路也在此設工具棚，亦受鐵路推動之故。工具棚房旁有碼頭，這一些土地屬樂居家族所有，因而稱這地區為樂居港（Lockeport）。這三位小商人都是中山人，他們知道在工具棚工作的大都是華人，在此附近開設宿舍、賭館和酒吧當會有足夠的顧客，事實果如所料。

三位華人小商人在樂居經營生意，距汪古魯鎮不遠（在其上游約一里），並不因此而成新埠。其後於一九一五年之大火，整個汪古魯鎮的華埠毀於一旦，本來有大批中山人和四邑人聚居，火災後，大部份中山人移居樂居港（其餘均留下重建華埠），以商人簡治平的父親為首，他資助九間住所的建造，並在此新埠開設什貨店，樂居港遂簡稱藥居（即樂居埠）。

居住於由簡治平父親提供經費興建的住所均是商戶人家，他們在一九一五年火災前，於汪古魯鎮的華埠都有生意。一九一五年後最初的五年，樂居埠發展緩慢，隨後定居這裡的中山人都很少，除了新遷入的中山人，便是原居於宿舍而在工具棚工作的中山華工。這一片土地都屬於白人，限於法例，華人不得購買土地，而樂居家族把此埠土地租給華人只根據口頭協議。

當一九二〇年蘆筍種植最蓬勃時，更多宿舍和各種生意迎合在蘆筍田工作的中山農工，紛紛建立。一九二〇年代，有些企業家在樂居埠附近設罐頭廠。在一九二五年南太平洋公司擴大此地的工具棚，結果使樂居埠發展更加迅速，在整個一九二〇年代期間的排華，樂居埠仍在成長。非法娛樂場包括賭館、酒寮、鴉片煙窟及妓寮都出現。妓寮由白人擁有及經營，而賭館、酒寮和煙窟多由華人經營，在樂居並無華妓，鄰近的汪古魯鎮才有。

一九二〇年代的樂居埠實在相當繁榮，那裡有華人擁有的影院，多年來放映黑白默片，中藥店賣中藥及提供中醫治療，六間餐館（其中兩間供應點心），九間什貨店（其中兩間並兼營屠宰場），一間磨粉廠及旅館以及許多宿舍，除了磨粉廠外，全由華人擁有和經營。磨粉廠由一名印度移民所經營，目的為迎合三角洲愈來愈多的印度人（農工）所需。樂居埠亦設有基督教堂，由浸信會主辦，從一九一九年直至一九四〇年代，希望根除罪惡的教會卻由罪惡金錢所維持，極富諷刺之言。事實上，當地賭館東主對於建立教會，是最為慷慨的善長。

最重要的雜貨店是元昌（Yuen Chong），原先在汪古魯鎮營業，於一九一五年遷至樂居埠，直到今日仍在。該店並非獨資而是合夥，股份可以轉售，在排華的日子裡，股本持有人使華工身份變為商人。元昌（Yuen Chong）是食物主要供應商，也是農工的重要信貸來源，且是樂居埠和汪古魯鎮一帶佃農合股經營的生意。自從一九四〇年代，三角洲的華人開始穩定下跌，該店已失去昔日光彩，但仍努力圖存，其他店號經已一一結束了。另一早期生意仍保存至今的是稱為亞鑊（Al The Wops）酒吧，由一位意大利人建立的，近來頗受三角洲農人和遊客所喜愛。

樂居埠的宿舍主要基於農工的需要，大部份農工都是中山人，而一九二〇年代期間亦有其他人如菲律賓人、日本人，有一個時期還有東印度人。農工可分為兩類：長工和年工或季節工，後者通常在農忙時雇用的。農忙時居於田間營棚，在空檔期間及冬季，多居於樂居埠的宿舍或其他主鎮。至於長工，他們或居於宿舍或在他們農田的住所。不論是否長期性或季節性的農工，在宿舍居住的大多在當地工具棚廠或罐頭廠兼職賺取一點薪金（很多罐頭廠的工作可用女士）。

除了各種正規生意外，樂居埠在一九二〇年代尙有多種曾提及的非法生意。妓寨不僅迎合白人也迎合非白人。賭檔均由華人經營，那時似有三檔，都歡迎白人和非白人光顧。在一般正常賭博之餘，所有賭館都經營中國彩票，每日開彩兩次，彩票均由餐館及其他店號經售，由於彩票隨處可買，使很多非華人覺得樂居埠有著無數賭檔。

一般華人，即使那些嚴額反對賭博者，都普遍覺得彩票是無害的，並無不道德之處。誠然，很多加州華人都認爲省會所定的反華人彩票法例是緊扣著排華運動。這種稱爲白鴿標的彩票，選用千字文中的八十個字作賭注對象，買彩票者可從八十個字中最少選買十個字。一九二〇年代平均每一元至一元半的賭注可買十個字。彩票公司（透過複雜的隨機方式）選出二十個字開彩，必須在此二十個字內買中至少五個字算賭贏，平均賠額由五個字賠雙倍至十字全中賠超過二千倍，華人的習俗是不論贏多少最後總要設宴招待親朋慶祝一番。

在一九二〇年代，多種社會機構都在樂居埠設立分會，該埠僱有看更，並成合作社以便和地主協商及管理用水。這裡的公共菜園始於一九二〇年代和一九三〇年代早期，而今居民卻在此種菜，每年盛產包心菜、豌豆、冬瓜和番茄等，或新鮮時食用或晒乾或送給親友。

在樂居埠所設分會中最重要的是俊英工商會和國民黨支會，有一間華文學校由當地商人資助，也和國民黨支會聯繫一起。汪古魯鎮的秉公堂包括了樂居埠，秉公堂在全美國都有分舵，那是一種秘密結合的會社，均與賭博活動有關連，和其堂號一樣，管制賭博不是唯一的活動，作為兄弟結義的秉公堂可填補沒有家庭生活的一般華人，並可傳播或引導國家民族思想，且可調解會員間糾紛，大部份樂居埠居民都屬秉公堂，故此這種排解功能極為重要。俊英工商會很多方面和秉公堂相同，例如像秉公堂一樣，使會員覺得有如自己的家，在總會裡設有娛樂場所及求職職業告示，這兩個機構都多次宴請會員。

秉公堂和俊英工商會也有不同的地方，例如秉公堂不限制任何華人而俊英會只限於中山人；秉公堂會員眾多，分堂遍佈各州，俊英會只局限於加州。俊英會也為會員排解糾紛及參與社團活動，但由於樂居埠均設有秉公堂和俊英會，後者的影響力及控制力不及前者。樂居埠俊英會最有效的是管制中山的包工和農工，秉公堂則在於其他一般的商務及在一九五〇年代前之於賭館。自從賭館衰落後，秉公堂亦隨而消失而俊英會仍存在。還有一點彼此不同的是俊英會不像秉公堂般富於政治色彩。

最具政治意識的並非秉公堂而是國民黨支會，樂居埠支會從一九二〇年代至一九五〇年代較為興隆，該會經費最初由簡治平的父親所供給，他領導汪古魯鎮華人在一九一五年遷到該埠的商人。

支會在孫中山先生訪問三角洲時，在華人間產生積極作用，一九一二年成為中華民國第一任臨時總統的孫先生，在一九一〇年前曾多次到此號召華人支持革命活動，由於他是中山人，該埠中山人響應特別熱烈。

衆所週知，中華民國的建立是多災多難的，領導民國的國民黨亦然。在美的國民黨向華人推展國家民族精神，並爭取他們的資助，美國華人經常捐款給黨，且在一個時期協助發展中國空軍。林燦士（Chaumey Chew）是樂居埠一帶的中山佃農，且是個相當成功的商人，在國民黨要求下，於一九二〇年代中期，協助中國購買數架飛機作爲訓練機司之用，在訓練完畢後，機司和飛機即可送回中國，該項訓練經已開辦了，但永不會完成，一個國民黨的敵人放火燒毀了購置才數月的飛機，全部飛機及存放飛機的機庫都焚掉。

國民黨支會在樂居埠一帶的另一項工作卻進展成功。一九四〇年代，中國展開新生活運動，努力於中國的現代化。在美國，這種努力表現於華文學校的建立，爲土生華人提供教育，傳播中國文化。在下午或晚間上課，訓練他們中文的讀、寫和講的能力，當他們在美國發展機會有所限制時，可回中國工作。樂居埠設有華文學校，和國民黨連繫一起，簡治平的父親是該校的最早創立者，後繼者是周崧，即國民一元商店（National Dollar Stores）的東主。該校由一九二〇年代一直開辦至一九七〇年代後期，甚少中斷。於一九四〇年代初期，就讀學生人數最多。

樂居埠支會另一重要努力是支援中國抗日戰爭（一九三一至一九四五），友援主要是經濟方面的援助。一九三七年保衛上海戰役中將領之一曾到三角洲一行，受到三角洲上各華埠的尊敬，他的光臨加強了華埠社團組織。

樂居埠和該埠的社團組織在一九二○年代最昌盛。一九三○年的經濟衰退打擊該埠，同時梨子收成不好（梨是園主要作物），蘆筍自從一九二五年便因某種植物病害而日走下坡。經濟不景迫使不少罐頭廠倒閉，一九三二年唯一的華人罐頭廠也因其廠主逝世而結束了，結果使當地居民失去了謀生之道，並使工人生活更不穩定。該埠不至於淪為廢墟，因為到處情形都一樣，甚至其他華埠更惡劣。很多以前未幹過農工的也來此埠或其他地方找工作，工作並不隨時可找到，工資下跌，生活水準下降，該埠努力掙扎求存。

一九四○年代，情況好轉，工資上升，普遍經濟較佳，失業者很少，以農工為生的都找到工作，二次大戰的轉機加速這種趨勢，不但由於一些農工被徵召入伍，且日本人多被拘留，遂造成更多工作機會給華人。

然而，三角洲華人人口已逐漸下降，在一九五○年代下降最快。年青的美國華人也投入政府工作行列，由於接受較好教育，甚少留在農田，而在一九六○年代他們的父母及其他老一代的移民已屆退休之年。即使排華在一九四三年終結，並無新的華人移民到三角洲以代替老一輩的農工，很多老農工都遷往城市和他們的子女一起，有些已逝去，有些留在三角洲靠微薄的養老金或社會救濟金過活。樂居埠真正衰落了，一九七〇年後期，大概只有一百人居住而現在人數不足五十人。

前曾提及非華人從一九二〇年代亦居於樂居埠，今日的非華人人口約十二人，多為白人。該埠的中山人約四十人，更夫早已不在，秉公堂和國民黨支會也於多年前關閉。至於商店，元昌貨店（Yuen Cheong Grocery）和數間白人商店仍在經營，迎合遊客觀光。如果不是由於一位新地產發展商和加州及地區代理的一場爭論，該埠恐已寂寂無聞而告遺忘。

論爭是由一對香港夫婦的地產商而起，他們成為該埠地主並企圖使該埠變為牟利的紀念名勝區，在此計劃未展開之前，首先是沙加緬度縣，跟著是加州政府均插手干涉，認為發展商的做法不能接納。政府策畫者主張州政府應為公眾及樂居埠居民著想，應對該埠加以保護和管制，保留該埠原貌，紀念華人對三角洲的貢獻。既要維持本來面貌而又不破壞樂居埠，誠是進退兩難。當其時的居民寧可被遺忘而得享平靜。

樂居埠的何去何從，聽由處決，似乎不當，變通辦法卻有極大差別：或任其繼續衰落；或重建為歷史活現的古跡；又或完全改為半商業化的市郊，象徵著華人文化和貢獻。目前，仍未有那個方案最優勝以作最後決定。樂居埠依舊是中山農工和佃農退休之所，白人也散佈其間，一個每逢週末供遊人乘車迎視的小鎮，一個位於沙加緬度河邊的小埠，它的古舊房下不及街道已給四週的梨園和沼澤所環繞。畢竟如何，樂居埠始終是美國碩果僅存的華人鄉鎮。

第五章 三角洲中國農工和佃農的每日生涯

遠朔自一八六〇年代中期，農業已是沙加緬度三角洲的主要職業和生計。初期農作物以穀類為主，一八七〇年代，種植水果和蔬菜更為有利。在一九二〇年和一九三〇年代，最重要作物是梨、蘆筍、洋葱和馬鈴薯。今日，除了蘆筍外，其他仍是重要作物，尤其以梨果為最。

早期三角洲的農田面積廣闊，地主無法耕種，於是僱用農工或租給佃農或兩者同時進行。在收成季節，需要農工更甚，就是佃農也需僱用若干農工，農忙最高峰時，經常好幾千農工在田間工作，華人佔農工人數很大的比例。

華人農工均在果園和菜田工作，人數隨時間而不同，其他農工如日本人、菲律賓人和墨西哥人都有被僱用。本世紀以來，在經濟不景氣時期，於收成季節華工人數最高可達二千人，超過半數是農工，其餘是佃農，大部份是中山人，他們都在果園工作（也有例外的），且大都居於樂居埠。

這些來自中山的農工，除少數是長工外，其他都是季節工人。在夏季，不論長工或季節工均忙於剪枝、除草、滅蟲和收割。冬季的長工便從事織籃（以便夏天收割之用）、修梯、擠牛奶和修護果園等，這些工作可使他們每天忙上十一至十二小時。通常他們分組工作，由一位兼通中英文的工頭率領，他並負責招聘、發薪、協商工作條件以及傳達僱主的指示。僱主供應農工們住所（如帳棚或床舖平房等），而工頭則供膳食。

至於佃農的工作稍有不同。大多夥同他人而為佃農，向白人地主租田，所租的田若是果園則種植水果，倘是菜田則種植馬鈴薯和洋葱。樂居埠居民及來自中山的華工，大部份雖長於果園，但多源自果園。收獲後，佃農分部份收益給地主，這種田租合約最初均是口頭協議，其後文字的租約較普遍。地主以供應化學產品及農具作為回報，有時更提供信貸（華人社團亦提供信貸）。同時，地主也關心農作物的發展及市場價格。

摘水果和噴殺蟲劑均用人手，為此，梨樹之大小以最易於修護為原則，農工剪枝時要因應用梯的空間，以便在梯上能伸手可及果樹的最大範圍，中山農工限制果樹的一定高度，使摘果工人在最高枝幹上可採摘果實。剪枝在確保每個果實因有充份陽光而均勻成熟，把過量果實切除使餘下的獲得充份成長。經過剪枝工作，梨子長得更大更完美。在機械化未廣泛採用前，噴殺蟲劑用的是十尺長的竹桿筒內裝銅管，唧筒和噴劑槽把殺蟲劑噴射果樹各處，剪枝工人整飾不規則枝幹以免妨噴劑工作。

三角洲上的中山農人和農工盡責而耐勞，灌溉果園（常指大農場），他們從日出工作至日落，灌溉農田分段進行，他們所用方法均學自中國家鄉。佃農們經年累月地工作於田間，使農場不斷改良。一九二〇年代，大部份農作均學自人手。拖運則用驢馬，直至一九三〇至四〇年代，才開始使用卡車，那時佃農和農工的生涯較現在艱苦得多。

農工和曾為農工的佃農都忘不了一九一〇年代的困厄日子，那個年代的工資不過一美元一天，有些甚至找不到工作。至一九一〇年代，情況稍為好轉，一天十二小時，工作可得一元半甚至一元七角半，可是工作常不穩定，一年工資在二百元至五百元間最為普遍。一天工資達一元半的已不復有，直至經濟大衰退時期的後期才再恢復，但從一九四〇年開始，工資已告急遽上升。黃有是位退休農工，他居於樂居埠超過半世紀，他所記的日記對那個時期的工資有詳細的記錄，據他所載，在一九三八至四一年，二次大戰時期的經濟有所改變，他的工資由每天一元半至約三元，差不多上升一倍；不過，在此期間，他一年工資只增加了百分之廿五，一九四一年全年所得是七百三十八元五角。

二次大戰導致農工薪酬有很大改進，黃有每年工資從一九四二年以來從未低於一千五百元，而在一九五〇年代中期更高達三千五百元，扣除了房租和膳食費（樂居埠的農工一年的

表一　黃有一九五九年的日記顯示他全年在
各項農工所花的時間：

工作編號	工　作　項　目	全年所花時間(小時)
1	除草	952
2	灌漑	589
3	剪枝	577
4	運果	337
5	剪枯枝	190
6	運枯枝	106
7	運送牲畜飼料	101
8	修補籃、箱	88
9	運送籃、箱	77
10	看更	64
11	運送樹枝	59
12	植樹	40
13	撐枝	40
14	爲油燈添油	40
15	疏通泥工	37
16	除去影響果樹生長的枝桿	24
17	修理梯階	24
18	運送木材	21
19	施肥	21
20	園工	18
21	棄置廢物	14
22	運送梯階	9
23	修理廁所	5
24	剪樹	4
25	收割小麥作爲雞飼料	2
26	雜項	3
	總計	3,414

表二 黃有一九五九年的日記顯示他每月的工時及工作地點:

工作地點	一月	二月	三月	四月	五月	六月	七月	八月	九月	十月	十一月	十二月	總工時
果園 1	101	81	160	262	134	218	248	204	157	287	192	124	2,168
2	107	78	50	33	88	47	46	75	161	37	40	50	812
3					88				5				93
4				5	24	28	30	41	31	24	89		272
5					5								5
罐頭廠						23	31	10					64
總 計	208	159	210	295	315	317	353	319	359	360	256	263	3,414

數目顯示小時

果園 1 是黃有的主管要工作地點。

高峰收割期(四月至十月)顯示黃有工作勤勞,不但在五個果園,還在罐頭廠工作。

膳宿費約一千元),在一九六七年他退休前的十年間,他的收支大概維持在這個水平。

即使工資有所改進,工資額仍十分低,很多農工均要節衣縮食,他們要交稅,寄錢給中國的家人,並且盡量把餘下的積蓄起來。他們要設法抑制自己不往賭館賭博,賭博對很多農工來說,誘惑實在很大,黃有是其中一個能自我節制的,他的生活儉樸(他的衣服和傢俱都極之有限)。

在一九五〇年代和六十年代,他平均可把工資收入的百分十五至二十匯往香港的家人,而儲蓄平均可達百分之五十。

農工們的積蓄到底怎樣？大多農工在中國買田起屋以便他日安享晚年（一九四九年中國共產黨執政使這些投資化爲烏有），有些用作回故鄉娶妻，有些用於和他人合夥爲佃農，有些花於辦理親人來美，也有些投資於生意或在三角洲上置地。

三角洲的農工和其他加州農工一樣，都覺得由四月至十月這七個月的工作時間長和工量多，以黃有爲例，他日記所載：一九五九年他共工作了三千四百十四小時，這是三角洲農工的典型例子（試比較每週五十小時及一週假期，一年工作不超過二千小時），這三千四百十四小時的工作，其中二千三百四十八小時是在四月至十月這期間，所有工作並非在同一果園，黃有通常同時在兩個果園工作，在夏季時則做四個果園並在當地罐頭廠工作。直至上個年代，最少工作時間每天十至十二小時。黃有和其他農工經常於早上五時半起床打掃及吃早飯，六時到果園工作，有兩次小息（每次十五分鐘，一次在上午九時，一次在下午三時），午飯時間由上午十一時半開始有一小時半，黃昏六時或七時收工，有些時候是八時。相反，根據在樂居埠退休的華工說，墨西哥農工現時工作是八小時（由上午五時半至下午二時，午飯休息半小時）。

茶點休息時間頗爲特別，不少農工仍記憶猶新，周厚賓和鄭慶饒想起在茶點時間，每人都食鹹蘇打餅，餅內夾上一塊黃片糖，既廉宜又可增補體力，這種蘇打餅有如三明治也和塗上果醬的餅乾一般，茶點均由伙伕做妥及帶往田間。

農工在果園從事各種不同工作，尤以長工爲然。長工似乎不用幹收割工作，他們要幹除草、剪枝和去蟲等工作，並且還要運送所割水果往加工倉庫。這些工作已佔去他們日常工作的八成，而收割工作由季節工人進行。這些臨時工人，沒有一定的工作地點，都穿梭於三角洲果園或農場間，由水果收割情況而決定去留。

果樹生長季節時，長工最爲忙碌，一月至二月忙於剪枝，三月開始種植果樹及除草，四五月以灌漑爲主，從四月至六月，進行去除枯枝，七八月是爲收割時期，除了運送水果，還須支撐結滿果實的枝幹。黃有述說除草時還要噴射藥劑，剷除一種名叫約翰草（Jhonson weed），此種草之根既厚且蔓延迅速，影響果樹的生長，他認爲這種草，是由一位名叫約翰的從歐洲帶來加州種植作爲牧牛之用，由於那裡不再用作牧牛，該草遂成爲雜草。

至於除枯枝的工作，梨樹有時會生萎菌病，使果樹枯萎和凋謝，長工必須把這些凋萎枝枝去除，否則會蔓延最後摧毀果樹。

冬天季節，長工在果園置放油爐，如晚間氣溫降至冰點時便要燃亮油爐，使果樹免於過冷。同時，堆積於果樹的土壤如果太厚，必須挖掘土壤，使空氣、水和肥料易達根部，這也是長工的工作。

　此外，在果園四週要種植大量樹木作為防風；當這些樹木長得過大而妨礙果樹，則要砍掉樹幹，這些工作均由長工負責。

　為期長達兩個月的收割季節，農田和果園均需要大量臨時短工協助或補充長工的工作，數以百計而有些時候更超過一千人以上群集三角洲，紛紛受僱為短工。樂居埠僱用數百臨時工人（尤其是中山人），或在假日時，聚於樂居埠的也數以百計。具有知識水準的工人（高中和大專學生及成人）都在試圖向包工尋找散工。在工作期間，這些季節工人便居於農場裡果園中的工作營，林值超（一位包工的兒子）在高中時的夏天都在這些工作營附近工作，他對這段生涯具有清晰生動的描述。林值超大約在十二歲便學習駕駛車輛，他通常跟隨他父親到各個工作營。當他年紀較大時，他駕駛貨車把廚房必需品拖到營地，那是他父親曾告訴他要在那處建立工作營。有兩次使他印象難忘的‥一次是在士路屋（Slough House）的位置上所建的採准花營，另一次是在碧加士（Biggs，近於Chico）那裡所造的圍欄。往碧加士（Biggs）那次的路程最遙遠，他駕駛了很長的時間，一直沒有時間休息，路面情況惡劣，很少車輛往來，當天他回到家時已很晚了。

　貨車把所有廚房應用品載往營地，這些用品包括食物、鍋和爐及其他等，由於工人均用柴，他們需要自己造爐架。每隊工人人數達三十至四十人，他們要有一個全職廚子，他需要為工人們準備一日三餐，無暇兼顧其他工作。由於冰箱難得，林值超每週數次運送糧食和必需品往營地，廚子要自行列出所需物品，營地沒有電話也沒有其他聯絡途徑，每次廚子需要什麼便只有告知林值超在下次送來。工人們並不自己舉炊，因為工作期間很短（不足兩月），而且他們要由一個農場做到另一個農場。通常新鮮疏菜等須每週運送數次，林值超也給工人運送他們所需的物件，例如中文報紙、郵件等。

僱用廚子（炊飯）在營地工作極具重要，如果今年的廚子不佳，明年便另僱個廚子。工人有時會對膳食不滿，包工便要辭掉廚子並即使改用他人。食用是最根本問題，金錢並非最受重視，大多工人所要求的不外是好的工作營地和滋養的食用。

工人付給包工的約一角五分一餐，好的包工要精打細算，不但不虧本還要使工人滿意。為了保持聲譽，林值超的父親從不吩咐廚子剋扣工人食用，廚子儘量用時令所盛產的食物，諸如豬肉蓮藕湯、菜干湯、苦瓜蠔豉湯等。有時於晚上更備有小吃（宵夜），例如雞蛋糖水或涼茶。

地主供給營地設施，每個帳棚足可住十人，工人睡在帳棚地上，而廚子則選擇陰蔽處作廚房，食物和工人行李存放一塊以便保管。

林值超還記得工人們雖然工作辛勞，晚間不忘娛樂，有些閱讀報紙或書信。大概百分之十年紀較老的在睡前吸口食鴉片，以求消除一天的辛勞。吸鴉片是非法的，他們則倒處於泰然。此外，有些工人在帳棚內賭博：擲骰子、玩骨牌、番攤及他中國賭博遊戲。也有不少工人每晚下棋，這種下棋玩意並無賭錢意味。有些工人懂得吹笛，這種樂器在中國很流行（林值超記不起有人會唱）。講故事也成為另一種受人喜愛的消遣，部份工人總愛圍坐一起聽說故事。林值超也聽說過一些周朝的故事，三王五帝的英雄故事，其中有位頗有學問的工人喜歡講述這些故事。有些時候，有人愛說鬼古使人害怕。中國鬼故事在當時相當流傳。大致說來，工人們所談論的都集中於他們的家鄉，他們對美國所知甚少，無從談論。

營地有時會發生疾病，由於工人都壯健，故不常生病，有病的不嚴重。他們工作雖辛勞，但營養和睡眠倒也充足。當工人受傷時，包工用貨車送往附近醫生診治。如果他們有病，大都自行用中藥醫治。廚子有時便像位醫師，如有人感到不適，他便給他另行烹調。

工人年齡從十八至六十五歲，很多都是獨身的，沒有受過什麼教育，他們需求單純，工作只求糊口。兩套衣服兩對鞋子即可過活。他們自行理髮，儲蓄或匯錢回鄉都是次要的，部份季節工人把所賺取的，毫不節制地花光於賭博，有些喜歡豪賭，有些只為了消遣，也有些輸光了的。

很多工人都極有節制和關心年青伙子，他們關懷林值超，並非因爲吸食鴉片時都叫年青人避開。同樣，他們賭博時也不願意孩子們賭博，年長的都覺得賭博是件壞事，即使他們仍舊賭，但勸諭後輩不應賭博。

在樂居埠住而從事農務的並非都是農工，很多是佃農。在一八六〇年樂居埠建立之前，很多華工都稱自己職業是佣人。一八七〇年，大多替美國農人做工。從一八八〇年開始，很大比例的華人成爲佃農，僱用華人作農工。換言之，幹了十年或廿年農工，很多已成爲佃農。自從樂居埠建立後，很多農工終生爲農工，有些從未有足夠儲蓄從事其他什麼，其他的例如黃有寧願做個農工，黃有覺得農工比佃農更安穩，他目睹不少佃農因失敗而虧去所有積蓄，且欠下一身債務，他並且說佃農須懂英文以便和美國人交易，須有經營農場經驗，與及具有找到工人工作的能力，他不願甘冒此種風險。

黃社貴（Henry Wong）當了十七年的農工，後來和他人合夥租田種植，成爲合夥的負責人，策劃一切農務，僱用工人剪枝和收割等，負起一切責任，即使做負責人可賺取較多金錢，但他覺得做佃農實非易事。多人合夥，情況複雜，彼此性格不同，有些較疏懶，有些較勤奮，難以管理，彼此性不合，有傷和氣。一年後，他辭去負責人改由另一人代替。

吳壽容多年來居於樂居埠，他做了差不多廿年的農工，他參加爲佃農，保羅依密（Paul Emmet）的農場有三百畝地，位於葛崙附近，吳壽容和他的夥伴在此種梨和蘆筍，所得利潤和依密（Emmet）逝世。吳壽容不大喜李作南（Lee Jok Nam）的經營，他認爲農場辦得不當，利潤太低。結果吳壽容做了負責人，他進行了很多改良果園的做法，頭一年的產量由一百噸升至一百六十噸，其後更增爲一百八十噸，他們在這期間都賺了錢，

吳壽容和他的夥伴合作了好幾年，直至合夥的負責人李作南（Lee Jok Nam）

在三角洲上成爲地主（農場主人）的爲數甚少，李采華是其中之一。方林彬初時只是一個農工，結果成爲農場主人，他的農場總部位於樂居埠附近，他受人愛戴，不但經商精明，且對果園獨具識見，憑個人經驗，在土地和農作物的經營均獲成功。使他成功的另一因素，是他屬下的工人（均爲華人）均把金錢存往他的戶口，由於他深受工人信任，甚少或不必向銀行借貸發糧餉給工人們，而且有廿至卅工人把工資交給他存放，他運用這些資金經商。雖工人每日所得不過一元七角半，但卅日即爲五十二元五角，卅人的款項每月達一千五百七十五元了。

工人如要匯錢回家或其他用途，他們可從戶口中提取。款項存於林彬，仍可獲利息。在

那些日子，華工把賺得工錢存放於僱主並不奇怪，他們視僱主如同銀行，僱主可能是包工或是佃農。工人們回中國省親時甚至委託僱主管理他們的積蓄。

方林彬在農場的成就不只限於財富（一九四一年他曾購置四百畝的良田），他努力教育子女重視勤勞的價值與種植的正確方法，他並且親自指導很多年青人如何種植及給他們汲取實際經驗。除了明白實際經驗的重要，還要正視正規的子女教育。他的兒子們都已大專畢業，所修習的學科使他們可應付今日農務所面臨的挑戰。

以方林彬的長子喬治為例，在購買所需農具以便增強運作的效率上，展露了他的設計之創新能力，他把設備加以改良以應所需。他誇耀自己把舊的番茄收割機改為貨架機，該機可以每次從貨倉載運八箱東西往果園。用水壓控制，具有不同速度，前進或退後均可，且在駕駛盤上裝置電腦，使司機不用離開座位而可知道前後輪是否一致。

周惠泉憶從述在韓戰時，他被徵召服役，因他是獨子，他兩次請求暫緩服役，在這延續期間，他父親請求方林彬給他一份差事，惠泉便被僱用了。在方林彬農場幹了兩年活，他和他的內弟梁占美（Jimmy Leong）希望自行經營農場，為了要向美國人租田，他們需要信用保證及財政方面的諮詢人，周惠泉向方林彬接洽並獲得支持，此事曾引起方林彬家人的不快。周惠泉在沙加緬度西部地方租田種植番茄，甜菜及包心菜。今天，周惠泉已是一個成功的農人，他的兩個兒子均繼承父業。

現在三角洲上務農的華人家庭不足十戶；都不居於樂居埠；可是，他們仍可和別人爭一日之長短，反映了近百年來華人對農業的貢獻。李朵華在葛崙擁有果園，號稱爲加州梨王，所種的巴力梨種（Barlett Pear）達一百畝之多；此外，他還種植番茄、甜菜、玉蜀黍、小麥和番紅花（Safflower），面積共二千五百畝，從十五個不同地主租借，他自己亦擁有不少畝地，在一九五〇年代，他的農場已達五千畝地；而三個孩子對農業都具興趣，使他甚感欣悅。

一般說來，樂居埠居民都覺得他們在三角洲所獲得的對待比加州其他地方好些，例如他們並沒有受到暴力攻擊。有些較年長的仍記得當地的稅務員，隨時會突然在餐館或農場出現，向華工徵收人頭稅（head Tax）。區開樞憶起那時的華工在農場用膳時，一旦見到稅務員，立即躲藏起來，檯上杯盤狼藉。華工都懼怕官吏調查他們的身份，即使人頭稅和排華在二次大戰時已告終結，可是當筆者訪問他們時，有些仍恐所提供的資料會引致官吏找他們麻煩（特別是移民官找麻煩）。

大體而言，三角洲的美國農人和地主都關心他們的土地和農產，他們深知農場是需要華工，傳統以來都對華人表示同情。華人和美國人沒有直接交往的以佃農、商人、包工和工頭

六六

居多，華工和美國人直接交往，因為他們不懂英語，而且工作和地點都不固定，他們又都由工頭或包工所監管，這些工頭和包工便成為華工和美國人的居間中人。

由於佃農和家人都居於農場，和美國人接觸機會較大，佃農的子女和美國農人子女很多時都會一起玩耍，有些農場地主由於喜歡他們的佃農，協助提供佃農子女和美國農人子女的教育機會，很多甚至提供佃農永久的租約權。

林值超憶述三角洲地區甚少華人男童和白人男童打架事件，可能由於華童和白童的學校是分開了的，只有在校際球類運動時，他們才互相接觸。

也有一些白人替華人工作。基利夫·史密夫（Cliff Smith）記得他拖運一袋馬鈴薯是五分錢，他受僱於華人拖運馬鈴薯，因為他較諸華人拖運得迅速，他有一輛貨車，駛往田間載運馬鈴薯，送抵碼頭再由船運往三藩市。（那時候的華人拖運工人仍善用馬車作為載貨工具。）基利夫·史密夫（Cliff Smith）說他和華人工作並無什麼問題。

在另一方面，曹格林（Joe Green）記起他的家僱有華人，在農場工作多年；六至八個是長工。他的父親租田給一位華人，那是他父親以前的同學，這位華人在葛崙經營一間雜貨店，同時租田種植洋，曹格林（Joe Green）且記得在果園之後有一所園工帳棚，每當夏天，他們便睡在地上，這樣較會涼快些。在睡棚內有一個煤油爐以便多天時取暖。他們做飯所用的是土製磚砌成的壁爐，架上一個大鍋，用木柴燃燒，天花板都被薰黑了和滿佈油烟。曹格林（Joe Green）偶然也會到那裡吃飯。在孩童時，他也有坐在馬車上，載滿著梨子運往河邊的渡頭，華工們都說中文，很少說英文，因為工頭要和地主交往。

曹格林（Joe Green）有他自己的佃農鄭森元（Sam Yuen Jang）他視為好友，鄭森元（Sam Yuen Jang）仍然在農場工作，不過由於患上關節炎，不能工作太多，他已做了五十年了。此外，曹格林（Joe Green）偶然也會遇上其他的華工，他們曾在他的農場工作，他亦被邀請參加在樂居埠的春茗，席間和他的老朋友們話舊，訴說別後的情形。

喬治亞當斯的祖父租田給華人，佃農是來自華埠，工作期間都居於農場，農場設有睡棚和廚房，地主告訴他們如何做所應做的工作，如果種植的計劃很大，三或四個佃農便要合夥參與。

喬治亞當斯記得那個年代，吸鴉片的很多；記起他的家曾有一戶佃農是兩兄弟，他們繼續工作至一九四二年，兩人均是單身漢，其中一人常受堂號追，有時他躲在喬家裡，逃避堂號的打手（hartchet men），他們會到喬治的農場找他。堂號的人甚至不理會亞當斯這家而逕行到農場找他們所要的人。（亞當斯這家從來不就此事報警，讓他們冷靜平息下來）。這一切都是一九五二年以前的事。此後堂號逐漸有所變化，較少粗暴。

喬治在長大的時期（一九〇七年至一九一一年），和他一起玩耍的都是華人，那是在葛崙，距樂居埠約十里。學校只在第一班至第三或第四班是隔離的，第四班後，全部在同一所學校。喬治說華人學生都是好學生，很多華人同學都成爲專業人才，他們的父母仍在農場工作，直至退休。作爲一個成人，喬治覺得大部份地主都反對排華法案（終止於一九四三年），他們喜歡華工且需要他們在果園工作。

農工和佃農的生涯實不容易，但並非十分苛刻。樂居埠的居民須辛勤工作，除了經濟恐慌時期，他們仍可生活下去，如非沈於賭博，他們仍可積蓄。生活方式相當健康，即使很多在三角洲上沒有家室，華工間彼此志趣相投，和白人相處也相當友善。他們可以從一個農工而成爲一個佃農或甚至位小商人或地主。

第二輯 華工的自述

第六章 一個農工、佃農和富農

——黃有、吳壽容、方林彬

此書下半部引介一些個人訪問，這些訪問提供重要而典型的史料。最感困難的在於決定誰應引介，每位被訪者都同等重要，在此向那些未列入此引介者表示歉意，但他們所提供的資料均已包括於前半部，同時在鳴謝中已寫上他們的名字。

這裡所提及的人都年過六十了，超過一半在中國出生，其他來自加州，均在樂居埠長大而在那裡長年居住，仍有一半以目前仍居於樂居埠，第六章引介的兩位，第八章的全部都是。差不多全部都是男性，只有兩位是女性。所引介的人物都或多或少和三角洲農業直接有關，其中有兩個事例是和工業有關，不過這些工業收益仍取決於農工和佃農的收益。

黃有（1900－1987）

我喚作黃有經已很多年了，出生時原名叫黃北盛，一九〇〇年生於距石岐約三里的員峰村。九歲時母親去世，由嬸母養大，父親去了北美洲。我在中國渡過了廿一歲，上過幾年學（那時的學費一年三元），做過一些不需要什麼技術的散工，例如種菜等工作，在十八歲時間開始學習木工，但並不喜歡這種工作。

我的父親步祖父和曾祖父的後塵，跑去美國。當他往美時已經四十歲了，他先往墨西哥工作，後來朋友告訴他美國的工作較多和工錢較高，他結果找到三藩市一間公司保證人到了美國，這間商號名叫金記，和金益及金山雜貨店一樣，可以僱用外來的華工。

父親經常提及要帶我到美國，他結果找到一位商人黃先生作保證人，給了他一千六百五十元，這個商人成為我的「冒籍父親」（Paper father），安排我和另一人（冒籍兄弟）一同來美國是做個學生。一九二一年我在香港乘「尼羅」（Nile）號抵達天使島，我隨身只有一箱的衣服和隻小木桶用作洗澡。

在天使島上有件事使我畢生難忘，那裡有個華人傳譯員號稱「老頭佬」，所有要問話的人都怕他，每人都認為他刻毒。聽說有兩兄弟，移民官知道他們來美前在家有一次晚飯，宰了一隻雞，於是移民官分別問他兄弟那隻雞的毛是什麼顏色，弟弟答是黃色而哥哥說是黑色，根據這些不同證供，政府便證明他們不是兄弟而把他們遣回。

我到美那個時候，移民條例經已有所改變，情況比以前較爲好些。我在天使島時，參加英語班學習英文，用膳時，每個人都在食堂進食，我沒有看見有華人打架或爭執。向我問話的通譯員爲人和善。移民官問我在家鄉住那間房，我兄弟又住那間房，家裡的傢俱如何擺置等，他們並沒有很多問題，只盤問了半小時，我和兄弟分別所提供的答案都一樣，因此批准了。問話之後，我須留在那裡好幾天，由醫生檢查身體，檢驗大小便，看看有否蟲病，但沒有照X光。

我離開天使島便往三藩市，幾個同鄉的來接我，帶我到樂居埠，父親沒來接，因爲三藩市的堂號有糾紛，我乘夜艇（果子艇）往樂居埠。

當我初抵三角洲時，我父親住在汪古魯鎮，那時候鎮上有很多宿舍，每天租錢是五角（包括一餐一宿和用水），房客不用立即付錢，可待發工資時才付款。我和父親便住在其中一所房子，每月房租五元，房子可放兩張床且有一小塊地方燒火做飯。當我們出外工作，我們在田間午膳，如不用工作便收拾些柴草在此燒飯。我們在此房子住了三年，直至一九二四年父親回中國爲止。

在這三年裡，父親替葛崙鎮金家（King family）工作，我最初沒有固定工作，能做的便做。除了在汪古魯鎮和葛鎮工作，有時也到盧大（Lodi）收割葡萄，並收割准花子，包工是廣生祥，他用車載工人往工地，大約是四十至五十人，我們住在牧場草地上的帳棚，雇主供應伙食並擁有廚子給我們燒飯，我一天收割准花子最高數量達六百磅。

幹了兩年收割准花子的工作後，便替另一個人工作了差不多十多年，來回於失打島（Sutter Island）和盧大（Lodi）之間，在失打島（Sutter Island）幹的是採摘水果、修剪果樹和灌溉工作，八月和九月份往盧大（Lodi）收割葡萄。十月份才返回失打島（Sutter Is-land）。

黃昏後，工作完了便沒事做，洗了澡和衣服便上床睡覺，有些時候會看看報紙，和我一般，其他華工都沒有什麼消遣，我們覺得工作已使我們滿足了。偶然在星期日，雇主會用車載我們到樂居埠或汪古魯鎮，讓我們可以逛逛商店或找些娛樂，有些便去賭博，而我去理髮或購些東西，偶而也會去看場電影，而有機會到鎮上實在令人興奮。有時我們只坐在行人路邊或聊天或看行人經過。農場所見的都是男人，經常見到的女人只有兩人，那便是雇主夫人和他的女兒，在鎮上可見到較多女人，我們通常逗留至夜幕低垂，雇主再接我們回農場。

終於在樂居埠定居下來。在一九二二年，該鎮已很熱鬧，那裡有兩間茶室，一間叫志英，另一間叫蘭亭，均售賣點心。最大的雜貨店是元昌（Yuen Chong），顧客可訂購新鮮的豬肉及燒肉，且負責送貨，一週三次，逢星期二、四及六。

我努力賺錢寄回中國和儲蓄，在經濟衰退時期，我的工資大概每小時一角，只要有工做也不在乎工錢多少，什麼工作都做，甚至沒有人肯做的也幹。假如一天賺一元，我仍可儲存，那時的生活水準很低，而我自己已甚少花錢，不抽烟也不賭博，唯一要花錢的是理髮，況且由於工作太忙，沒有時間用錢，每天只是工作、吃飯、看報和睡覺。直至一九七二年，我仍舊在清還父親為我移民美國所欠的款項。自從他在一九二四年退休回中國後，我還得寄錢給他、繼母和弟弟們。我於一九三五年回鄉娶妻，一九三六年再重返這裡，更加要靠工作維持在鄉的妻子和父親一家的生活。

所賺取的錢，一部份寄回家鄉，其餘便存於銀行，例如汪古魯鎮的亞歷士布朗（AlexBrown）、三藩市的美國信託公司（American Trust Co.）和市作頓（Stockton）的美國銀行（Bank of America）。從一九二二年至一九三五年，我整整花去了十四年才積蓄足夠的金錢回鄉。

我的積蓄尚可在中國置產，在一九三五年回中國之前，已寄錢給父親買了一所房子居住，當我回鄉時再買七畝米田，每畝田四百元（約一百二十五美元），總共用了二千八百元

（約八百零六美元）。一九四七年第二次回鄉時，從父親買回以前所買的房子，另外給繼母買一幢房子和一些耕地，這次還買了一畝荔枝園，花了九百元（約二百五十九美元）和十畝水稻田用了一千元（約二百八十五美元）。

一九四七年從中國回來，又再在葛崙工作。一九五一年到了樂居埠工作，從一九五一年直至一九六八年退休為止，都是替丹尼士理尼（Dennis Leary）工作，偶然在工餘時到別的地方工作，我住在農場，走路到汪古魯鎮工作，因為雇主不提供交通服務，路程大約半小時。

如果工人要求提高工資，老闆不願意，於是便從中取巧，他加工資五角一天但同時也提高工人的伙食費五角，我們認為這樣倒可以獲得較好的食用（由一間糧食公司負責農場的食用）。可是當星期日不開工時，我們沒有工錢但仍要付給所增加五角的伙食，結果我們仍舊是損失。雖是如此，老闆對我們也不錯，他富於幽默感，即使我們並不大明白他的言語。

工作期間，工資是根據工作時間計算，雨天時，不能工作便沒有工錢。

父親退休後回中國，他再娶，妻子和我的年齡相若，我的兄弟和她相處並不和睦，父親想把我買給他的房子留給她，但兄弟們反對，要求他出售，我知道他們難於相處，便由我買回，把錢給他，分成七份，兄弟雖獲得分發，但仍住在那裡，而繼母不願和他們一起，我在一九四七年返鄉時再給她買了另一幢房子。

我在一九三五年首次回鄉時結婚，那時妻子只有十六歲，親戚們安排一切，在石岐一間照相舖映了一幅全家福（包括父親、繼母、兄弟、內妹及同父異母的弟弟），這幅照片現在仍掛在廳的牆上，也大排筵席，宴請親朋戚友，那是我一生中的一件大事，有那麼多人參加，實在使人興奮。

和新娘相處很短的日子，我需離開她回到美國謀生，養活妻子、家人和自己。生活擔子重了，我更加要工作，而且把四十年來所積蓄的都差不多花掉了。

一九四九年共黨執政時，妻子到了香港那時候我沒有足夠的金錢帶她來美國，由於新政權，我已失去在中國所有的財產，而我已近五十歲了，很多華人都開始在這個年紀退休了，但由於中國的改變，我不能回鄉退休，況且已一無所有，唯有先在三角洲繼續做農工，打消退休念頭。由於和妻子分開這麼多年，我們沒有孩子，我經常寄錢給她，使她生活不缺。

一九五七年，我有了一點積蓄，回到香港，那時我們收養了孩子，買了一層樓給她們居住，並非一幢獨立的房子，而是一幢樓宇中的單位，當時香港的樓價仍不算貴而美元匯價很高，那層樓位於較好的地點，價錢是七千美元，有三房一廳，妻子和孩子住一房一廳，把其餘兩個房間出租，幫補孩子的學費和生活費。

一九六七年中國文革也引致香港的騷動事件，香港政府未能採有效措施，經濟衰落，樓價狂跌，那時房子不易出售，但由於政治局面不穩定，我要求妻子來美，請了一位律師辦理移民手續，同時要她來美前把房子賣掉，最後以四萬港元售出，比十年前購買時少了八千元，即使是損失了也沒有別的選擇，只要能賣掉便是，我不想一九四九年在中國失去了的資產再次發生，誰會知道香港到了一九六八年會怎麼樣？到了今天，但願不曾賣掉，那層樓至少值了廿四萬港元（當黃有說及此事時，他對筆者面帶笑容，對自己的決定並不後悔）。

一九六八年，妻兒來了美國，孩子足十一歲了而我已屆六十八，我退休了並遷出農場，在樂居埠買了一所房子居住。

由於我已退休，我須注意開支，妻兒並不習慣這種生活，和在香港所過的不同，他們在中國或在香港都不用工作；也不知道我的生計。在香港，別人都羨慕他們，有丈夫和父親在美按月寄錢回來，他們多幸福！現在他們看見我的境況和所幹的工作，怎麼賺錢寄給他們過活，我一生節儉而他們習慣於揮霍。習慣上我始終是小心如何花費，這樣便和家人有所磨擦，結果妻子在收割季節時到罐頭廠工作，以便賺取多些零用錢。後來我發覺她在樂居埠過得並不快活，數年後，她聾了，在一九七八年逝世，給一輛往屋後退的垃圾車撞死的。

我的女兒結了婚，移居加拿大，兒子正在上大學，他並不常來看我，我計劃回中國探望兄弟和親戚們，希望和兒子一起同住。

吳壽容 (1897－1984)

我生於中山縣東村，從一九五九年便居住於樂居埠。十多歲時在叔父果園工作，他種植很多種水果如桃、李、荔枝、枇杷、香蕉、橙和紅橘等。那時候，在中國難以謀生，糧食不足，工作短缺，做農工一整天的所得不過一角，而我已很幸運了，有親戚僱用。基於這種原因，很多都決定離開家鄉到外國另謀生計。

一九二〇年，我已足廿三歲，決定往外國，就我所知，那時有三艘船載運乘客，由香港駛往美洲大陸，那是中華號（China）、尼羅號（Nile）和南京號（Nanking）。南京號是其中最大的一艘，我遂乘搭此船，船上大概有一千華人，約五百人前赴古巴，五百人往墨西哥，不足廿人是到美國的。

我從香港出發往墨西哥，付了八十元的船票，船是開往三藩市，船程足足花了卅個白天和夜晚，抵岸後，被送往天使島等候往墨西哥的下一班火車，因為我不是往美國，所以不用接受移民官的盤問。

在天使島逗留了十天，那裡拘留著大概有八百華人，很多是四邑人，有男人、婦女和小孩，我仍舊記得很多不合理對待華人的事件，記得一個守衛在飯堂高聲呼喝：吃啦！飢餓的人群在擁往飯堂時幾乎互相踐踏致死。食物只有少量粗飯。飯後被推往圍有障礙物的地方稍作休息，在那十天，我聽到很多自殺的事，有些被拘禁達三年之久。我覺得美國人不把我們當人看待，華人來此只是和家人重聚，但遭受如同囚犯般的待遇，很多情形和移民無關的也成為不准入境理由。我還記得有一個同鄉在那裡住了三年，他稍懂些英文，幫助新抵達的填寫表格或寫上姓名和地址。我覺得自己幸而不直接往美國。

在天使島渡過一段悲慘日子後，我終於從三藩市乘火車往墨西哥的墨西加尼（Mexicali），華人稱此地為新花旗，我們在那裡所獲的對待較諸美國，具有人道得多，我停留了十八個月，那裡有華人團體和同鄉會等幫助初到境的華人，我加入中山同鄉會，那裡沒有房屋，所有華人都住在帳棚，每個同鄉會有自己帳棚的地方，我被安置在一個足夠兩人居住的帳棚，如果沒錢，店舖會記帳，稍後償還，有些供膳直至找到工作。我們抵達後翌日，邀請到一所茶室午膳，茶室有各種點心供應，並且叫我們送個訊息給家人，使他們知道已平安抵達，會社有人協助辦理這些事情，並由一些可以募捐的每人出五角。那裡的雜貨店，有華英、意志英和意大利等商號。

墨西加尼只出產棉花，也是剛成為產棉區不久，那裡氣溫炙熱，夏天早上超過八十五度，下午更高達一百一十度，縱使天氣酷熱，我們華人農工並無其他選擇，只有在田工作，也是唯一可提供給新入境者的工作。我在一間棉花公司找到工作，是在田間工作的，每日工作十小時，從早上八時至下午六時，採摘棉花一百磅可得三元所摘棉花放入一個長袋，這些袋堆疊在馬車上，運往製造棉紗的地方，棉籽作提供食油之用，棉產品運往美國。棉花種植園從美國銀行獲得款。

最初，棉花的價錢爲每磅五角，可以維持大量工人的工作。第一次大戰後，棉價由於需求量少而跌至每磅一角，很多從事此種經營的都告破產，有些華工甚至沒有工錢發給，因爲並無其他工作，很多華工打算離開而另謀出路，不少意圖到美國去。

一九二一年左右，超過八百華工從墨西哥境偷渡往美國，一些非法組織從事這種勾當，每處都有美國偷運者，我們華人需付款較高價錢給這些機構，以便獲得入境的機會。偷運入境三藩市的代價是每人五百元，不保證安全。由於互相競爭，這些偷運公司之間有時發生糾紛。在偷渡每一個過程，都可能被攻擊。被殺或被拘捕。犧牲者往往是無知的華工，他們只是爲了謀生而已。這八百華人之中，有些被殺了，有些被拘捕而遞解回中國，有些安全到了美國。

我付給一間美國偷運公司五百元，實際上是由我的親戚孫社才支付，他是我的保證人，在葛崙工作。我在早上六時從墨西哥上船，安全地抵達三藩市，他接船並交錢，然後我們再乘船到沙加緬度，那時候，並沒有公共汽車往沙加緬度，我仍舊記得在船上工作的一位華人水手。

抵達葛崙後，我最初做農工。江鏡寬（Kong Geng-Hoon）是當時的工頭，由他負責和僱用。我夏天採摘水果，冬天修剪果樹。

一九三〇年當赫伯特胡佛總統（Herdert Hoover）在任時，經濟開始走下坡，三角洲的華人難有一份全職的工作，多數只能找到兼職工作，為期三至五星期，之後又再另找工作了。人們拚命幹任何工作以求生存，有些以釣漁糊口，他們所捕的多是鱸魚。

華人情況一直並無好轉，至富蘭克林羅斯福（Franklin Roosevelt）當總統時，華人才獲得社會福利法案的保障，工作也比以前較多，可是華人仍需辛勤工作，那時的工資率是一日一美元（包括膳食）而工作時間是每天十一小時。

那時有些華人在美國人的大農場做佃農，一般農場的地主供應所需的農具和維修，而佃農只提供努力，所獲利潤大多均分，但也有佃農獲不公平對待，例如一些地主只把百分之廿五甚至廿的利潤給辛勞的佃農。

在經濟衰退時期，我沒法在果園找到工作，為此，我便在元昌雜貨店（Yuen Chong

Marker）工作了一段日子，直至二次大戰爆發，日本勞工給徙往營地，對華工的需求才告增加。而且，軍方徵募了很多農工，政府更鼓勵非法居民參軍，這是改變自己身份的機會，所以我也想從軍，被徵召爲1A隊，但元昌（Yuen Chong Marker）的老闆要我繼續給他工作，並提高每月一百元的工資至一百零五，我不答應，除非每月有三百元，否則不幹。我覺得這是我的機會，如果放棄了這個好機會，以後會一輩子窮困。同時又有人找我去做農工，這次並非散工而是做佃農，是給保羅依密（Paul Emmet）幹活，我認爲戰爭時期的糧食會提高，決定離開元昌（Yuen Choug），和他們組成佃農。

保羅依密（Paul Emmet）在葛崙附近的農田約三百畝，種植梨子和蘆筍，他同意提供所有設備和所需物品而我們供應勞工，利潤五五分帳。我們幹了數年，直至其中一位合夥人李作南（Lee Jok Nam）逝世。這期間的利潤極少，李先生工作數十年，他堅持所做的是對，我們都聽從他。不過，我發覺耕種得不當。李先生去逝後，依密（Emmet）先生要我繼續工作，我告訴他會進行很多改變果園種植方法，他並沒反對。

當李先生經營時，他在四至七月時不另澆水，那時果園產量約一百噸，很多果實都不大，並未充分成長。在我負責果園之後，按個人所知的方法管理，例如四至七月灌溉三至四次。此外，我了解中國和美國氣候不同，中國夏季氣候濕且熱，日夜氣溫差別不大，而這裡三角洲熱和乾燥，日夜氣溫相差較大，種植方法不能一般無異，況且，葛崙的果園面積寬廣，中國的果園零散而高低不平，築有很多排水溝排去過多的夏雨，有時建水閘控制水量。由於氣候和種植知識匱乏，那時中國的水果產量和這裡比較相差很大。能在這裡工作，我深感欣慰，工作的成果使人難以置信。在我經營後首年的產量由一百噸增加至一百六十噸，隨後更增為一百八十噸，價錢為每噸一百元，這是我的機會，那個時期，老板和我賺了些錢。

老闆希望當當縣長。他舉行結婚卅五週年慶典，邀請很多人參加，我和其他華人都在內，在慶典上，他當眾宣揚如果不是我給他工作，他不會有今日這個盛典，那時刻，我深感榮耀。

由於他的一席話，我便為眾所知，不少果園主人都願意我給他們幹活。

此後在葛崙一帶，我逐漸有了名氣。有些華人妒忌我的成就，找些美國人寫信告發我吸鴉片，老闆把這些信給我看，我告訴他每逢四月至七月期間，我便患有花粉熱病和哮喘症，如果不吸食鴉片便不能耕作，雖然有服藥防止這種過敏性疾病，但沒有效。吸鴉片並非我的習慣，廿年來只是為了治病，過了七月份便不用吸食。依密（Mr. Emmet）先生聽了我的解釋，並沒有取消我們的合作。

我為保羅依密（Paul Emmet）工作了差不多廿年。在一九五七年，離別鄉井已達卅七載了，年屆六十歲仍是個單身漢，我到香港結婚，翌年妻子來美和我一起，在葛崙再住了一年；那時候，老闆和他的妻子相繼去世，果園也出售了，有些人仍舊叫我給他們工作，但我決定退休，遷往樂居埠。現在我有兩子一女，全部進了大學。這年是一八八〇年，在這三角洲一帶渡過了六十年的生涯。

方林彬（1893－1958）

沿著沙加緬度河的三角洲，仍舊繼續務農的華人家族中，方林彬家族是其中之一，方林彬（一八九二至一九五八）雖去世，他一手所創的農場仍由他的三個兒子繼續經營，農場總部位於汪古魯鎮的賽車路（Race Truck Road）。

方林彬的生平事蹟由劉炳允所提供（劉炳允乃方林彬生前的管工）。方林彬為人謙恭有禮，待人坦率，而且勤奮儉樸備受農場工人及其他人士所信賴。由於他經營有方，結果他購置了差不多四百畝良田，便是今日他兒子所耕種的農田。

當方林彬年輕時，用冒籍入境方法從中國進入美國。有人說他於一八九三年生於三藩市。他的祖居是三藩市華埠，一九〇六年大地震時焚毀。方家遂遷往沙加緬度。方林彬在那裡渡過少年時代，後來他到葛崙工作直至一九一一年。

方林彬刻苦奮鬥，他從農工而成為佃農。在經濟恐慌時期，沒人願意賒食物給他，曾經因沒錢交電費而給終止電力供應。其後情況好轉，一九三九年，他購入一九六畝農場，成為最大的華人地主。一九四一年，他再增購二〇一畝，除了自己所擁有的農場，他更租賃數百畝農場，使工人和機器能充份工作。

林彬不但精明且通曉農事，所經營的農場十分成功，他種植甜菜、玉蜀黍和梨，都獲利甚豐。住在農場的工人主要有十人，農忙時，僱用超過七十工人。林彬僱用的工人，廿至卅人均信任他，把他們的工資都存在他們的帳戶如同他們的銀行一樣。林彬能夠有資金買地的原因之一。

華人通常不輕易信任別人，如信任便完全信任。工人們信任他，他不需要向美國銀行借款，利用工人存放的款項經營，不必發工資給他們，直至農忙之後才連本帶利發還他們。那時工人每日所得不過一元七角五分（那時一瓶牛奶是一角，一條麵包售一角；而且林彬供應食宿）。卅天的所得即達五十二元五角，廿人至卅人的所得，每月則有一千五十元至一千五百七十五元。

工人們如要匯錢回鄉或寄東西返家均須自行辦理，這是方林彬的管理規則。林彬請求劉炳允幫那些不識字的工人們寫信，他們所收的信也由劉炳允讀給他們聽。同時劉炳允負責監管工人，記錄他們的工作及工資，處理逢星期日發工資的事。他們要清楚記載誰要給工資及誰不給而存於林彬的帳上，因為是管工，享有稍多的休息時間，且在年終時獲林彬的年償

（花紅）。

林彬同他的妻子於一九二九年到加州，他們有六個孩子，他都十分愛護，雖然他的事業有成，但他希望他兒子們能繼承他的事業。他的三個兒子都已大學畢業，長子主修管理學且熟悉農場新設備的機械操作，次子畢業於加州大學（載維斯分校）農科，現在三個兒子分工合作，長子負責機械運作，次子主理耕種農作物，第三子掌管人工事務。

林彬逝世時已六十五歲，把遺產都分給六個子女，兒子們再向他們三個姊妹購回經營權保留產業的所有權，這樣較易於處理事務，否則家族的農場主人太多，難於管理，他們組成了林彬父子公司（Lum Bunn Sons）。

周惠泉曾和林彬共事，他回想起林彬為人良善且教了他不少農耕的事。林彬不辭勞苦地教他和其他各人剪枝和包紮工作，與及種植果樹的正確方法；再者，林彬不理會別人抱怨他花去太多時間教授年輕工人如何工作。周惠泉在林彬農場提供信貸及財政方面的諮詢及證明，他向林彬洽商，林彬不顧其家人的不滿，一口答應了他的請求。

第七章 三角洲裡長大的下一代華人

——鄭慶饒、林值超

鄭慶饒·（1917－1983）

雙親在中國中山出生，於一九〇一年抵達美國，主要是在三藩市的洋服店工作，也有兼做其他工作。姊姊在一九〇四年出生，一九一七年我生於三藩市。一九二三年姊姊十八歲時出嫁，婚後遷往葛崙和她丈夫一起，那時我只得五歲，跟他們住在一起。

姊夫名黎寬（Lai Foon），他結婚時年屆廿八歲，在葛崙務農。他工作的果園位於格蘭島（Grant Island）的河畔大樓（River Mausion），那裡正是每年舉行盛大集市的地方。姊姊、姊夫和我便住在那個農場的農舍，農舍由農莊主人建造，為農工們預備飯食，姊夫在田間工作，他負責僱用和監督農工剪枝和收割。

我在葛崙上幼稚園，每天上學都坐學校汽車，偶然趕不上校車，便坐周莉莉（Lily

Chow）（婚後稱陳莉莉）的女兒，他耕種一個小農場。跟了姊姊一年，她有一個時期也是上同一間學校，是鄰居周宇關的女兒，

數年後的一九二九年，姊姊和姊夫停止農耕，遷居樂居埠，住在第三街，房子近在周厚賓現在所住的附近，這時，我又回到樂居埠和姊姊一起，那時的樂居埠是個十分繁盛的華埠，尤以收割季節為甚，很多人群集此埠，而我則就讀於汪古魯鎮小學，那裡認識了很多朋友，例如（周厚賓的弟弟）是我的好朋友之一，他大我一年，在葛崙出生，他有三兄弟和兩姊妹，喬治、湯尼、斯旦里、羅絲和碧寄（Becky）。我們年幼時的遊戲主要是跳舞、彈吉他和玩麻雀牌，學校也有舉辦舞會而我們都踴躍參加，那時候的舞多是慢步舞，有時我們到沙加緬度看電影，到沙加緬度是輕易的事，元昌雜貨店（Yuen Chong Market）的僱員經常要往那裡購貨，我們便跟他們一道往沙加緬度。此外，我們也喜歡一同在樂居埠碼頭的河邊釣魚和游泳。

在我十二歲的夏天，我開始替一位農夫叫黃中球（Wong Chung Kau）工作，他的農場在樂居農場附近，也是我舅舅陳錦（Chan Kum）（商店東主）的好朋友。由於這個緣故，我得以在他的農場工作，幹的是把梨子分類，這種工作多是由婦女、老婦及年輕小伙子做的。有六至八個工人在包裝部工作，每年都僱用同樣的工人回來包裝水果。他們均富有經

驗，工作效率高，雖然可用機器，但大部份的工作還是用人手。農場在河岸有自己的貨倉和碼頭，貨倉同時又是包裝部，有路軌連接農場。

在收割季節前夕及包裝未開始前，包裝部的工人忙於預備工夫，例如做貨運箱子及標籤。水果收割了用貨車或馬車載往貨倉，工人便把水果放進機器裡沖洗，再由機器轉動的輸送帶運往圓盤以便分類，一些工人站在輸送帶旁把壞的水果拿起，水果給分成大、中、小三種，然後分別放進箱裡包裝。工作由早上六時至下午六時，有時要加時工作。

並非所有農場都有自己的貨倉和碼頭，那些沒有包裝設備的便交由包裝公司代理，姊姊在其中一間大的包裝公司服務，她是一位水果包裝工作的女工頭，有些人叫她未婚的姓名鄭瑞娥，也有些叫她黎寬 (Lai Foon) 太太。那時她在一般女華工當中頗負名氣。她會說英文，常替華人和美國人傳譯，很多華人靠她翻譯，他們去看醫生時也請她做傳譯。她的丈夫 (Lai Foon) 只稍懂英文，她對他的農務和其他工作幫助很大，有一個時期，他們二人在樂居埠正街 (Main Street) 開了一間酒家，後來他們夫婦遷往洛杉磯。

當我替黃中球 (Wong Chung Kau) 工作時，他已四十多歲並擁有一個很大的農場。除了農務，他還要料理工人的食宿，他僱了一個伙頭，我還記得這個伙頭吳壽容，他燒得一手好菜，我在樂居埠住了兩年直至小學畢業（那時的小學，由第一班至第八班）之後，我回到三藩市繼續唸中學，每當暑假，我大都回到中球（Chang Kau）的農場做工。

由於我不再是小伙子了，不用做包裝工作，而到田間摘梨，那是相當辛苦的工作，要一個人背負一把頗重的長木梯，每早六時早餐後，三或四人一組便出發到田裡，每人背著一個籃，爬往梯上採梨，我們要採摘那些差不多大而成熟的果子，不能隨便採摘，所以在每一個地點不會摘到很多梨，於是爬下梯來，把梯移到別處再爬上採摘，由於木梯很重且是A字形的，不能摺疊，至少有十二尺長，搬動時要份外小心，否則很容易倒下，摘滿了一籃水果後倒往箱裡，箱子倒滿了，馬車便會把它載走。天氣很熱，特別在下午更甚。我們除了午膳外還可休息兩次，一次在上午九時，第二次在下午三時。在小息時，坐下喝茶和吃些鹹餅乾，餅裡夾有一小塊中國的黃片糖。那時候，差不多所有農場的工人都吃這些做點心，大概是便宜吧！況且一片黃糖可補充體力。茶點由伙頭準備好了並帶到田裡。

夏天在中球（Chung Kan）的農場工作時也住在那裡，還記得住的地方是二層樓，樓上用作休息和睡覺，樓下是飯廳。平日晚上都留在屋裡看報和其他人聊天，我們很早便睡了，八時便就寢，且很快就睡著，鼾聲很大，週末，一些工人到樂居埠，我是工人當中最年輕的。

記得有次夏天替黃中球（Wong Chung Kau）的親戚黃中發工作，他叫我到蘆筍田去除草。就我記憶所及，做這種工作的人並不多，我也不明白爲什麼他要用人手去除草，也許有人知道原因，在炎夏中，整天彎腰拔草，我感到極之辛苦，所以做了三天便放棄了。

有一年夏天，我在汪古魯鎮的一間商店工作，店東是一位黎先生的，除了招呼一般顧客外，還在店中收彩票，這種中國彩票和李糯（Reno）及他浩湖（Lake Tahoe）賭場的彩票（Keno）相似，中國彩票不用數字一至八十而用八十個不同的字（李糯（Reno）和他浩湖（Lake Tahoe）等地的彩票源自中國的彩票）。我替買彩票者寫彩票，也因此而多學了八十個中國字。買彩票者都是農工，也全是華人。那時很多華人商店都附設這種服務，作爲賭館的分館網，發售彩票，但經營彩票的是賭館，人們不必走往賭館買，每日開彩兩次，我知道很多商店都加入這個分銷網，只在夏天經營，那時候很多華人聚集於樂居埠和汪古魯鎮。

三藩市的中國大學生也到果園工作，他們並不需要認識在那裡的任何親朋，往農場工作成了他們的傳統，也許他們覺得那裡的環境和城市不同，當然也有些人是爲了賺錢。去果園工作包含了賺錢、渡假和田園生活，當我憶起那些夏天的日子，雖覺有趣，但那種生活並不舒適。

此外還有一件有趣的事，是關於看更的班炳（Ban Bing），我不知道他姓什麼，只管叫他做班炳（Ban Bing）叔，他並非眞的是我的叔叔，中國人習慣上稱大一輩的叫叔。在那段日子裡，我回樂居埠都在三藩市乘船的，沿途停泊多處才抵樂居埠，並繼續駛往葛崙和沙加緬度。我通常是坐下午六時那班船，到達樂居埠已是凌晨一時，班炳（Ban Bing）叔便來接到我叔叔的商店，他負責樂居埠的夜更，可能是一些商人僱用他做安全警衛，他的職責是在夜間巡行，攜同一條木板及木棍，邊行邊用木棍敲打木板，按時報更，凌晨一時便敲打一下，二時便二下，餘此類推，直至五時。在中國的鄉村，據說也是這樣打更的。在加州的樂居埠，早期仍有打更的習俗，那是富有趣味的。

在三藩市中學畢業後，我便再沒有到果園工作了，距今已有四十年了，而今卻再提起。現在我並沒有後悔我所做的，我樂於在田間工作，仍記得樂居埠的一些人，但他們都告退休了，農場都由新一代用新的設備去經營，可是我在田間工作的日子，永遠難忘。

在這個訪問中，不少人和事都在腦中閃過。

林值超

我於一九〇九年十月九日出生在葛崙，有兄弟姊妹多人，我是家中長子。曾就讀於葛崙的華文學校，上課時間逢週日下午五時至九時而週末則在早上。在校成績優良，不論是在華文學校或是美國學校，我都是優異生之一。由於我經常和祖母相處，上中文課時很易掌握，很快便可明白每個字的意思，即使現在還不能寫很多中文，但仍可閱讀中文。在一九四○年代後期，我在州政府當稽查員時，我曾再進修中文，那是工作上的需要，現在退休多年，對中文又再逐漸忘掉了。

葛崙有兩所公立學校，分別為東方的學童和白人學童，早於我入學前已建立的。為東人辦學校，因此當地人口中日本人和華人佔相當的比例，我在此校完成小學，跟著升讀的那間中學均有白人和華人，我畢業於那間中學，仍舊記得那時的同學，有些至今仍健在，例如鄭添（Tim Cheng）、鄭榕森和鄭羅文（Norman Cheng）等。

年輕時候，一些年紀較大的同學和白人同學打架，他們不在校內而在校外打架。在三角洲一帶，很少真正打架事件，但在三藩市，華人和意大利人便有很多衝突，華人絕不到意大利人的地方，意大利人亦然。三角洲一帶的學校甚少這種爭執，因為他們都被分隔開，就是放學返家，雙方都沒有往來，唯一大家在一起的機會是校際運動比賽，學生家長和朋友都來觀賽，很少美國土生的華人喜歡參加的，我卻和白人同隊伍，大家都知道那時候種族的問題並不多，種族歧視仍未見明顯。很多白人來到葛崙的華埠尋樂，對華人並無歧視，來的以農人和他們的子女居多。種族問題在城市較多而在鄉村較少。鄉鎮的屋與屋間相距很遠，彼此不易相聚，即使有糾紛存在，也都屬於些微不足道的事情。

我的中學生活是愉快的，加入的校隊常獲冠軍，學業成績優良獲老師喜愛，每月的成績都榜上有名。和白種友伴相處和洽，覺得和他們能夠打成一片，也常到他們家裡留連忘返，和他們混在一起多於和其他中國人，甚至還約會學校的白種女孩子。

後來在加州大學（Berkeley）攻讀電機工程，但並沒有畢業，因為我認為那時候在這方面難有就業機會，所有兄弟姊妹都曾讀大學。

一九二八年離開三角洲便進大學，暑假又回到農場工作。經過了多年的大學生涯，我受僱於周崧（註：周崧是國民一元商店（Dollar Store）的創立者及東主，生前曾是美國最富有的華人。他慈善為懷，尤喜捐款給華文學校。）的國民一元商店（Dollar Store）該店初設於三藩市，後來擴展到沙理拿（Salinas）、摩達士度（Modesto）、長灘（Long Beach）、洛杉磯、西雅圖。砵倫（Poorland）及其他地方。我和周崧家人素稔，周崧生長於沙加緬度，洛家父知他頗深，他精於經商，業務由沙加緬度拓展至三藩市及他城市。在經濟恐慌時期，他仍僱用很多華人在他六十間的店舖工作。

一九四〇年因病入院治療，康復後回到葛崙，重建祖屋並在那裡住了約五年。在葛崙期間，正當日本人被逐至拘留營期開始，我從事農務，因父親並無購置任何田地，我租了三年的田，接收了三個日本人的農場，這些日本地主都被政府徙往拘留營。那時候，一位好朋友梁關六（Leong Kwan Luk）協助我的農場工作。

在經營農場期間，農作物的價格完全受制於罐頭廠，他們制定價格，如果他們不需要我的作物，根本便不出價，我極表不滿而離開那裡。一九四六年遷往少加緬度從事生意。

當我在葛崙那段日子，州政府需要我協助移民局的工作，家父在聖若瑟學校（St'Joesph' s Academy）唸書時認識的一個人後來當了三藩市移民局長，他希望家父能協助他，因家父熟悉三角洲一帶。可是家父不幸於一九三七年逝世，他遂到葛崙找我到移民局工作。

在傾談中，知道該局有意整頓三角洲上華人的身份，那裡約有一千三百華人的身份仍未明確，我答應替他工作，但條件是不得控告任何身份不明的華人，最後同意重新調整而控告，這樣遂受僱於政府司法部，協助處理三千個個案，工作上的困難可從以下一個例子說明：依據僞造文件及出世紙，一位婦人竟有超過三千個孩子而且都是男孩，案件延續至父親及祖父等輩，案情委實錯綜複雜。

最後，官員發現一位美國律師和一個華人印製假文件，每份文件平均收取三百五十元，律師得二百五十元而該華人得一百元，但此同夥的華人售出的牟利高達一千元，他們利用同一個城市的同一婦人作爲那些冒籍入境者（即買紙仔）之母親，此二人終於被拘留，當我爲周崧工作時，曾於金門書院（Gdden Gate College）習了兩年法律，在控告他們時，我提供四至五人作證；為此，三角洲一帶的華人身份得以整頓。

我的父親祖父都住在三角洲地區，關於祖父的情況都是從別人口中知道的，祖父在我出世前已去世了。

一般人都稱我祖父叫亞超，美國人卻多稱他為超先生，但他姓林。他來加州約在一八五四年，那時他大概十五歲（中國歲應是十七歲），他跟很多和他差不多年紀的人一起來的，最初去當金礦工人，由於其他礦工的態度使華工難以立足，他於是離礦場到三角洲上找工作，除了農工外，一八七〇年左右的築堤工作也提供不少就業，吸引不少金礦的華工。即使築堤工作辛勞，至少工作較穩定，工作營地隨著築堤進展而向南推移，華工聚散於小埠胡德（Hood）繼而葛崙，在德明先生（Mr Deming）的聘請下，我的祖父開始在他的農場工作。

那時華人在那裡建了兩幢房子，他便和初到美國的祖母住在其中，他在果園當季節工人，同時也經常替德明先生在葛崙的農場工作。

祖父定居於三角洲後，他乘帆船返中國結婚並攜同妻子回來，他的第一個家在胡德鎮。

祖父極受德明夫婦及其家人歡迎，他們曾說過終其一生都歡迎我們這家在他們的農場，兩家人來往甚密，我則誕生於該農場的。

祖父有三子，均出生於葛崙。長子出世時，德明夫人替他取名燦士（Chauncey），頗著

英國氣息的名字，因她是英國人。他除了叫燦士（Chauncey Chew）外，更加上中國的姓〃

林〃字在中間，他便是家父。

德明夫人很關心父親的教育，那時在三角洲上入學實在不容易，那裡附近沒有學校，於是送父親到一間半私立學校，名叫聖若瑟學校，位於理奧威士打（Rio Vista）他在那裡接受正規的英式教育。他在那校讀至畢業，相當於高中程度，然後回到德明家的農場，他並沒受過中文教育但能說流利的中文。一九〇五年，他和黃雪倫於三藩市結婚。

家父在德明家的農場作佃農，以收獲分酬的制度。那時代，三角洲上除了家父，甚少華人精通英文，由於他能操中英文，白人地主常向他諮詢，並請他向華工們提供各種不同農作物的種植，諸如准山田及葡萄。他也種植一些新的作物且是多方面的先驅。和一些華人合夥，從事一項艱巨的冒險，在一個從未有人種植過的島上種植洋蔥、馬鈴薯和其他蔬菜，這項工作需購買大量拖拉機及其他複雜的耕種設備。經過三至四年後，整個農業普遍不景氣，迫使父親和他的合夥人賣掉所有農耕，父親得以轉危為安。一九一五年，不再耕種而從事農務包工的工作，他為准山田、葡萄田及果樹田等提供農工。很多樂於惠顧因他很快即可召集卅至四十農工，不論是收割或種植又或修枝等均可；再者，他有自己的貨車載送工人，使他的包工服務更受歡迎。

他從事包工服務後，由德明農場遷往葛崙，相距約四分一里。他的弟弟仍留在農場。在葛崙建有房子足供一家人居住。在鎮上他並經營其他生意，包括一間什貨店和冰淇淋店，和人合夥開了一間餐館及投資於賭場。葛崙的華埠頗大而繁盛，主要是中山人，直至一次大火焚毀了部份華埠，大多華人才離此而往三藩市。

一九二七年，父親在葛崙開設暑期學校，讓那些願意其子女習中文的家長可以送其子弟入學。就在我們的房子撥出部份地方作校舍，電源也是從這所房子供應，在園子裡放置些桌椅。學童約十人，父親請了個教師，學生每月也繳交學費作為教師的部份薪酬。該校維持了大概三年，後來葛崙華埠已設立了自己的華文學校。

中國革命之父孫中山先生於一九一一年前，曾多次到訪三角洲，尤以在葛崙為甚。孫先生的革命事業，家父是其中一位積極支持者，他獻出了不少金錢，是革命空軍軍需的代辦人，用農場後面沒有樹林的一片空地，作為機師訓練場所，他由眞臣公司（Janson Co.）購入第一次大戰留下的戰機，除了購買飛機外，更捐錢給孫先生的軍隊。

機師來自葛崙、檀香山、西雅圖和砵倫（Portland）的年輕華人，他們到其他城市接受最初的訓練，然後到葛崙的農場考驗射擊，他們並可駕駛飛機，一位美國人叫艾德華做教練，他訓練他們飛行，修理飛機及拆卸零件等。

機師們在農場上訓練了多月，並住在為他們設的營裡，家父為他們貯藏那些飛機，一旦需要隨時可以運送，他等待運送的命令，但那些飛機永遠不會抵達中國了，因為給人蓄意放火燒毀了（約在一九二九年至三○年），那是我第一次看見父親流淚。那次火災在當地報紙也有報導，但華人從不透露所燒毀的是些什麼。

第八章 樂居埠的主婦、賭錢日和終老

——訪問方婆婆、何蘭清、嚴在民及區開樞

方婆婆（1905－1986）

從一九三〇年代便居於樂居埠。於一九〇五年一月一日生於中山大環村，在一所基督教學校讀了四年。一九二〇年代，此校男女學生超過七十人，那時代已算是很不錯了。讀的雖是基督教學校，但我並沒受洗，對聖經所言，深信不疑且認為所有宗教都勸人為善的，在學校所習的英文並不多。

父親是一位商人，在歐洲工作。祖父曾當縣長，其後任駐古巴大使，我是一個中等家庭的傳統婦女，我的婚姻也按當時習俗由父母決定，出嫁時是十六歲，事前並不認識丈夫，他的中文姓是黎氏，居於美國而回中國結婚的。我們在中山共同生活了一段日子，買了些田耕種，後來他返美開始在三角洲工作。一九四〇年因二次大戰，我賣了田地移往樂居埠和丈夫

一起。那時的樂居埠早已有了商店、雜貨舖和餐館了，很多華人在此居住和工作，孩子們在此上學。我的兩個兒子都在盧大（Lodi）出世，一個醫生從盧大（Lodi）來樂居埠載我去盧大（Lodi）並給我接生，休息了四天便回樂居埠繼續工作，自此丈夫和我更辛勤地工作。

那時，很多華人都在蘆筍包裝公司工作，包裝工作是把蘆筍捆紮成束及打包，有時也兼做裝運工作，例如把一包包的蘆筍運往附近的碼頭等待船運。我們沒有固定工作時間，如有大量蘆筍運到，便要早上五時起來工作，若某些日子的蘆筍不多，我們下午才開始工作。由於只把當日的蘆筍包裝，到了傍晚已有足夠的時間把工做完。通常二月和三月是最忙的月份。在四月，我們不在包裝公司做而去埃靈頓（Isleton）的罐頭廠。不單大人做工，孩子們在十一歲或十二歲也做工，他們下午四時放學後便幫父母工作。丈夫和我都在罐頭廠工作至九月底；除了這些工作外，還有其他散工，例如包裝梨子及其他水果，每天工資一元七角五分。十一月和十二月，我們也有種植些洋葱和蒜頭等。

罐頭廠多僱用華婦（註）。婦女日間工作時，可把小孩留在一所屬於該廠的特別幼兒所，那裡有人照料小孩，不用另外交費的，該廠還提供宿舍給工人，租錢是每週二元。如一個工人在廠做滿若干期間（通常是一年）。這些租金便退回給他或她。可惜，該廠因某些原因而結束了，影響不少樂居埠的華人，他們不得不到沙加緬度找工作，但由於不懂英語，無法和美國人溝通，使他們不易受僱。

註：該罐頭廠爲趙寬（Thomas Foon Chew）所有，他是一位美籍華人。該廠常用能說中文的做管工，對於在廠內工作的華人特別照顧。

在罐頭廠工作時，我丈夫在一次意外中給機器輾斷了手，出院後，他不能繼續工作，保險公司認爲是他的過失而不負責賠償，他只有從政府領取救濟金。自此之後，我一個人維持一家生計，什麼工作都做，艱苦地撫養兩個兒子，後來丈夫也逝世了，那是一生中最悲傷的日子，但我提起勇氣振作起來。一九六九年，兩個兒子都進了大學而且都能畢業，現在都有一份不錯的工作，我引以爲傲。六十二歲時，我便退休了，在樂居埠安享清閒平靜的晚年。

目前有女孫四人，分別是十五歲、十四歲、十三歲和十一歲，男孫一人。他們聰明伶俐，對我很好，全都是幼子所出，長子仍未婚，很多人包括親戚及中國鄉下的人都曾提過親，但他要自己決定。

我喜歡回想早年做農工的軼事，記得有一次在一月份，要做得很晚才把洋葱種好，那時很冷，霧色朦朧，有些工人燒些柴草取暖，其中有個站得太接近火堆，結果背部著火，他沒有燒傷，回想起來到是一件十分有趣的事。

政府把我的房子重修並供給一個新的火爐，雖然我的兒子有間較大的房屋，但我仍舊喜歡在樂居埠獨居。這裡和在中國所住的鄉村十足一樣，彼此都相識，一同工作，我們互相幫助得以生活至今。

何蘭清（1897－1980）

我丈夫名叫歐陽漢強（Owyang Hong Kerng）而我婚前名何蘭清，英文稱爲周喬太太。

丈夫生於中山大良，我則生於張家邊村，距石歧約三里。周喬十歲便到了美國，他在三兄弟中排行第三，他們都在美國工作，也死於此，孩子們都在三藩市和沙加緬度。周喬十年前去世，那時他已屆九十歲了，我現在八十二歲也忘記很多關於我丈夫的生平。只記得他常回中國，有一次回鄉和我成親，我結婚時是十六歲，在那個時代，一個女孩到了十八歲還未結婚便認爲老處女了，所以通常都早婚，結婚後他便回美國了。

婚前，祖父不讓我和其他女孩上學，他認爲女孩子上學是沒用的。我只學習煮飯和田間的工作。一九三〇年代中日戰爭爆發時，我來到美國，那時丈夫是個農夫，我便幫他在果園工作。後來因虧本而停止務農，他做工人而我在罐頭廠工作，是蕃茄、蘆筍和桃的入罐工作。通常每日工作十小時，日薪是二元五角。也有在碼頭的包裝工場幹稱重量及包裝新鮮蘆筍的工作。工錢是一包蘆筍一角。包裝場裡塞滿了人，相當擠擁，每人都很忙碌，有時在傍晚也工作。

我有兩子兩女和十個孫子，他們都住在三藩市和沙加緬度。我獨自兒住在樂居埠，這裡我有很多朋友。

嚴在民（1903－1988）

一九〇三年生於中山東濠村。童年和青少年都在香港渡過，父母受過良好的教育，祖父頗富有，我得以專心讀書而不用工作。當我仍在香港求學時，父親在美國警局做傳譯員，祖父和叔父等人早在一九〇〇年代便去了美國，他們經營女服裝店超過七十年了，祖父去世後，叔父和親戚們繼續經營了好幾代。

一九一八年，我十五歲時和很多鄉人一同去了美國。本來計劃在父親的時裝店做裁縫。第一次大戰時被徵召入伍，戰後回來，自己經營一間裁縫店（位於三藩市基利街GearyStreet），只裁縫訂做的女裝，僱用一些推銷員接訂單，由於生意並不好，結果結束了，那時候很多店舖都相繼結束營業。

結束了裁縫店後，我遷往樂居埠，其實我從未幹過農活，也不適合於戶外工作。到了樂居埠，我只是休息，釣魚過日子。後來開始在罐頭廠工作，做了一些日子後便回中國結婚。

回鄉後，鄉人介紹妻子給我，後來才知道岳丈曾居美多年，婚後才和他熟悉的，早於一九二〇年在樂居埠彼此見過面。一九二〇年代，我常去樂居埠，該埠相當熱鬧，記得曾有個時期，一些朋友勸我到樂居埠當農工，我當時拒絕了，因爲我從未在田做過工。

一九四五年，我返回樂居埠找工做，仍未能找到合適的工作，我既沒有在美受過教育也不懂農活，終於在賭館裡工作，最初對賭館一無所知，只是站在那裡假作賭客，那份差事，週薪約二十元，所賺足夠生活了，也別無他求；再者，這份工也是臨時性質的，一旦不用上工便去釣魚。很多人包括菲律賓人、美國人、華人和日本人都到賭館賭博。我在賭館做了一年半，直到它被法令所禁而關閉了爲止。初時，很多小鎮如樂居埠都不受法例管制，後來都一一受管治了。

停止了在賭館工作後，友人介紹到罐頭廠工作，工作了兩年，積蓄了些錢，家人也來到美國和我一起（約在一九四七年）。生了兩個孩子後才在樂居埠買了這間屋，以前是間酒吧，屬於陳天信（Tin Sin Chan）所有，建於一九一二年。我購於一九五〇年，差不多所有酒吧都結束了，當那些美國酒吧東主逝世後，也沒有人再開酒吧。樂居埠裡大部份的房屋都是華人建造的，而我的房子都是美國人所造。我選此屋不在乎它的外觀，只注重它的內表。當我買下此屋時，廚房有個很大的冰箱，後來把它搬走了。住在這裡已超過了卅年。在此不用交稅，因爲我是個退伍軍人。

我的孩子們都不懂中文，他們並沒有機會學中文（他們的中學不設中文科）。我擔任樂居埠俊英工商會義務秘書差不多卅年，平日有練習書法，朋友們常叫我給他們寫字。現在年紀老邁，不再理會這些了。想起往日在樂居埠，對於別人的事情，我倒樂於助人的。

四個孩子都在樂居埠出世。當他們出世時，我仍在罐頭廠工作，工錢少，生活很苦，而幸那時的物價不高，而我力求儉樸。長子十二歲便去送報沙加緬度蜂報（Saeraments Bee），每天可得五仙。冬季經常下雨，我便駕車送他，因他還不能騎腳踏車。這樣要花去一元一天的費用，但常常下雨，有時整個星期都下雨。一次早上四時他醒來，對我說：「又下雨了，真不想去送報了。」我告訴他：「孩子，**繼續工作**，這是你的責任，不要輕易放棄，要堅持下去！」而今他已卅四歲了，他一直在政府工作了十多年，便是這個道理，如果在孩子年少時不好好的教誨，當他們長大了便不會聽從你的。要讓他們知道父母的經歷，他們才會懂得勤奮。每逢夏天，所有的孩子都在包裝工廠工作，賺取他們的學費，即使他們都獲得獎學金，那仍是不足的，都需要在暑期工作。

有些父母買玩具給孩子們玩，而我卻買書給孩子們看。早期買了很多書刊，一直保存至今，連同他們學校的用書也都存放在孫金煥（Sun Kum Mun）先生的房子裡。由於自己在美國並未受過良好教育，能夠做的便是買些書給他們，希望他們從書本中學習。我給他們購了一套百科全書，他們有什麼不明白的都可以自己去翻查。

長子英文名是史迪文・雷孟德。女兒名莉莉，獲加州大學戴維斯分校法律學位，現於沙加緬度工作。兒子在高中時很活躍，也是學生會的通訊員。

今日的社會，文學遭受輕視，科技則深受重視。早年大家講究中國文學，有些時候，當我寫白話文便不得不用古典文句表達意思。年輕時，我喜歡寫詩，並投稿到報章。我曾投稿往三藩市的金山時報（Chinese Times），用洛居在民筆名發表了三首詩。那時候只是興之所至，現在覺得實在是貽笑大方，正如中國一句成語所說：書到用時方知少！即使如此，我仍繼續不時寫詩，但不再在報上發表，只作個人寄懷怡情吧了，主要的還是因為有人叫我寫點詩。

記得那年兒子和女兒一起高中畢業，我給他們題了首詩，儘管自己文學修養不足，也得塗鴉一首：

生朝七十年二長，

客久他鄉是故鄉；

事業已隨流水去，

雄心空托岫雲茫。

莫嫌紅葉秋容瘦，

但願黃花晚節香；

總算兒曹知努力，

名題碩博莫徬徨。

洛居在民

一九八〇年十月卅一日

區開樞 (1894－1984)

家父是夏威夷農工，在我抵美國前已逝世。他送我入學（在中國）。雖只讀了兩三年，已感慶幸。那時年幼，所學並不多。年紀稍大便去了香港，到處玩耍，無所事事，後來和一些朋友到了美國。

在一九一五年乘西伯利亞號（Siberia）抵美，大部份的乘客都是華人，爲數約二百人，有些去美國，其他則往古巴。單程船票是六十元，我唯一的行李只是一個箱子的衣服。

抵達後，我逗留在天使島整整一個月，有些同伴停留達半年之久。在島上，親人有來看

第八章　樂居埠的主婦、賭錢日和終老

一二一

過我，僥倖未遭受像其他早期華人那種不善的對待，移民官並沒問很多話。

樂居埠大部份的華人，和我一樣都是來自中山縣的，也有些來自四邑。來美前我已結了婚，在樂居埠定居後，便到了果園農場（Orchard Ranch）那裡一個美國人的農場做工。留下家室在中國，一個人跑來美國，到了一九二二年才回中國探望妻子，他後來遷往澳門，在那裡逝世，那個年代，沒有人攜同妻子到美國的。

在我第一次回中國時，順道去過夏威夷，在那裡住了十多天，回來後，我在李糯（Reno）的娛樂場做了一個短時期，後來又回到樂居埠的賭館工作。那個賭館是由四邑人經營的，他們都很好，汪古魯鎮也有些四邑人，那時賭風頗盛，汪古魯鎮有三間賭館而樂居埠則有兩間。

一九二〇年代，汪古魯鎮大概有一百至二百個菲律賓人，現在只有約十人。那時的賭客多是菲律賓人，也有些是日本人和美國人。招呼日本人好過美國人，當日本人贏錢時給我們較多的賞錢，最低的賭注是二角半。賭館從早上十時開到晚上十時，工作人員每工作兩小時便可休息一小時，早上免費供應兩餐。我每天連同賞錢的收入最少有二元，儘管東主給我們的工錢看來似乎算多，但他的收入遠遠超過我們的所得。

也不知道誰開始經營賭館，我知道簡炳（Charlie Bing Lee）擁有一間賭館，其他的賭館經常更換東主。賭館裡也有中國女性的工作人員。三藩市的歐陽士賓沙（Spaneer Owyang）是簡先生和地主樂先生（Mr Locke）的通譯員，他在汪古魯鎮出生並在那裡的中學唸書，先工作於三藩市的美國大通銀行（Bank of America），後投了軍，他的父親是經商的，住在樂居埠。

簡治平（簡炳的兒子）是我的朋友。他的父親曾在一間美國餐館任廚師，積了些錢，在汪古魯鎮起了一間屋，那幢房子不幸燒毀了，他遂遷往樂居埠。

這所房子是簡治平的，由美國人建造，以前是間賭館，現在成為一間會所，稱為快樂閱報俱樂部（The Happy Reading Club），在一九七五年創立。他為人和善，讓我們在這裡閱報。自從六十五歲退休後，一向都到此閱報和見朋友，早上常坐在會所外的板凳。會所有會員約十人，每人都有繳費，雖沒有選舉會長或幹事，但卻有一名理帳員。

閱覽室約一百平方尺，有一張木的板凳，由中國木匠造的，不用一枚釘，已超過六十年了，它漆上淺綠色。竟後有些菊花、柿子及金幣的木雕。室的中央有一張大的方桌，圍以椅子，上有一盞吊燈，在室的一角放有一張書櫃，櫃上是一本帳簿，櫃附近的牆上掛著一面鏡子和一些相片，牆上也掛著一個古老的大鐘和一個中國日曆。

會所訂閱三藩市的金山時報（Chinese Times），我們的經費也包括水電費的支出，並且舉辦每年兩次的宴會。平日的飯食甚爲簡單，但這兩次的飲宴卻十分豐盛，共有九個菜式，周秋是廚中好手，他駕車往三藩市選購上等的菜料，烹調這九道菜的宴會。

結語

該書講述廿世紀三角洲上華人的歷史──他們從事農耕，建立樂居埠，與及散居和退休的狀況。指出華人對加州農業貢獻，並評斥美國報章對華埠吸毒、賭博和賣淫的誇大及聳人聽聞的報導，提供了較清楚的歷史。

那個時期華人農工全是依靠勞動，限於依靠機械的操作。在極大困厄當中，華工的墾土種植，均有超卓的表現。他們所建立的良好農務慣例，促使收穫增高。他們對於所承擔的工作，辛勤而盡責。

加州農業發展爲商業化的過程中，華工之影響甚深。十九世紀中葉，華人所定之包工制，至今仍甚盛行。承包者給地主負責僱用及管理一組農工，地主直接和承包者交涉，不必和個別農工接洽，工資由工作件數決定，而非以工作時間計算。工作完成了，承包責任也就完結，農工即可離去，地主不用長年僱用。此制大量降低生產成本，對於農業化的成功，貢獻良多。

華人亦建立了加州的佃農制度，由數名華人合夥租田耕種，佃農交首期按金及若干成份的毛利給地主，通常地主提供工具和住宿，並且決定何種農作物，此外並負責出售作物及價格，佃農只負責種植和收割。此制可行且改善了華工的生活條件，地主和佃農基於互相尊重，相處和洽，佃農責任較大但較一般農工所得也較多。

華人經常也能自我發展，一八六〇年，大多華人只受僱於白人為農工、佣人或築堤工人。自從一八七〇年至一八九〇年，大部份華人受僱於華人佃農，很多且成為佃農。成為佃農所具備的因素有多種：具有十年甚至廿年農工的經驗，能懂英語，對農務運作有一定認識，有少量資本，和華埠有良好的聯繫，肯冒風險和負責任。一個農工如要出人頭地，具有社會及經濟地位，通常有三個途徑：成為佃農或包工或店東。並非每個農工都可躋身於三者之一。

據說一九四九年以前的華人都把大部份的積蓄寄回中國。可是在三角洲一帶的華人並沒這樣，在工作期間乃至退休回鄉都沒有把全部金錢帶回中國，從訪問他們所知或從他們個人紀錄及日記所見，部份積蓄是存於三藩市當地的銀行。有些農工存於他們僱主帳戶，只有一小部份的儲蓄匯往中國，約相當於他們所賺得的百分之廿至廿五。該筆匯款足夠維持在中國一家多口的生活，那些退休後返回中國的也沒有攜回所有在美國的儲蓄，仍舊存於美國銀行，或留在美國親友中作信託用途，此舉使很多美國農人大為驚異。

所訪問的退休農工，大多在排華法案實施期間來美的，華人移民不受歡迎，很多均持僞造文件，幾乎全都在聲名狼藉的天使島上經過嚴密審問，此事使他們談虎色變，不願再提，甚至和子女們也從來不說。然而，三角洲上的華人已覺得，自從一九四○年代，華人遭受的對待已告好轉，較之在大城市的華人，他們感到白人的敵視較少。打鬥和堂口間的交戰不再厲害。

三角洲上華人——農工、佃農、樂居埠居民、小商人、主婦和賭客——從他們的經歷都可追懷當地移民歷史舊事。面臨重大的障礙，從語言的屏障到資金的短絀，從種族的反感到思鄉，他們都在新天地中力圖一個容身之所。有些長久定居美國，有些居留數十載，只有很少數是作短暫過客，縱使他們微不足道，仍舊在鄉村地區安身立命，成家立室，對當地經濟作出了貢獻，地位得以改進，家人生活得以改善，成為加州重要的一份子，即使在困苦之中，他們力求實現心中的夢想，也是美國人的夢想——一個極富意義的想法，並且得以承先啓後。

附　錄

「假紙」的節錄

以下是黃有幾年前用來幫助自己以「假紙」的身份進入美國的節錄，我認為可使讀者更易明白當年華人來美的困難。

黃有個人資料：

我姓黃、名有，原籍中國廣東香山（今日的中山縣）。生於隆都鎮石嶺村。今年十九歲（所有歲數根據中國曆法計算），生於光緒二十九年八月八日（即一九〇四年）。

黃有的家庭：

我的父親叫黃財，生於光緒六年五月二十九日（即一八八一年）。我母親姓劉，現年三十九歲，生於溪角村溪角，離我們的村莊約步行一小時的路程，她有紮腳。我有一個弟弟，但沒有姐妹。我弟弟叫黃就，今年十八歲，生於光緒三十年十月二十日（即一九〇五年）。弟弟和我均未婚，我們從沒一起到過任何地方。

黃有的親戚：

我的祖父叫黃光強，他在一九〇六年去世我只有三、四歲。我的祖母為劉氏，紮腳，她於一九〇七年去世時我為四、五歲。我父親有一個哥哥，名叫黃繼，他沒有孩子，他於一九〇八年去世時弟弟和我分別是六和七歲。

我的外祖父叫劉森，我的外祖母叫彩，亦有紮腳，他倆均於我很小的時候便去世，因此我對他們不太了解。我母親有一個哥哥，名叫劉德文。據母親說，他於十七八歲時便離家去了安南（越南）。他從沒有回來過，現仍住於安南，今年約四十歲，已婚及已有孩子。

黃有住的房屋：

我的房屋很舊，向南，坐落於村莊的中部，不近海，但離石縣的海約兩唐里，屋子前面是稻田，屋後相一列屋子便是山。

我的屋子由兩個部份組成，約十八尺高、六十四尺長，中門部份約十二尺闊。屋子沒有側門、後門、內院或天窗。屋子週圍也沒有圍牆、亭閣、花園或後院。我們也從沒有在屋子附近飼養任何家禽。

ONE DAY, ONE DOLLAR

The Chinese Farming Experience in the
Sacramento River Delta, California

PETER C.Y. LEUNG
Asian American Studies
University of California, Davis
Davis, Ca. 95616

The Liberal Arts Press
TAIPEI, TAIWAN, REPUBLIC OF CHINA

Supported by the Overseas
Chinese Educational Foundation
1993

DELTA HERITAGE

BY PETER C. Y. LEUNG

A HUNDRED MILES OF LEVEE BUILT
THE TULE MARSH MADE FERTILE
GENERATIONS OF KNOTTED HANDS
WORK AND REWORK RECLAIMING THE LAND
FARMS AND ORCHARDS, GRAINS AND FRUIT TREES
MARK OUR LABOR
NOW THIS LAND BECOMES GRAND

HERE WE ARE
THESE CHINESE IMMIGRANTS
THE EARLY TENANT FARMERS OF AMERICA
OUR STORY UNTOLD
OUR WORDS SCATTERED
LIKE THE FRUIT'S FORGOTTEN SEED

ONE DAY - ONE DOLLAR
OUR MEMOIR
FOR THE BITTERSWEET STRUGGLES
OF A HUNDRED YEARS GONE BY

WHERE HAVE OUR DELTA CHINATOWNS GONE?
ONLY OUR PICTURES REMAIN
TATTERED AND YELLOWED
WAITING TO BE SEEN
OUR FORGOTTEN WORK
THIS PANORAMA OF DELTA FARM LAND

AUGUST 18, 1985, UC DAVIS

園延洲流泣立田年

田永美傳可確良當

闢績基罕歌功傾昔

廣勞奠民可前萬憶

壤果裔籍涯冊埠覽

墾穀華史生成華展

堤栽農見園涯域此

築勤工散田集流旨

梁靜源作于加州戴維斯大學一九八五年八月十八日

iv

Table of Contents

v

Preface

The history of California is the history of many different peoples. Much has been written about the various nationalities which settled the land: what they were; why they came; how they lived; and how they affected the development of California. The Chinese were among the first to arrive. They joined the great Gold Rush which began in 1849. A little more than a decade later, Chinese crews were an indispensible element in the construction of the transcontinental railroad. Chinese also played an important role in such diverse areas as fishing, garment making, cigar manufacturing, laundries, household service, lumbering, levee construction, and agriculture. Although San Francisco's Chinatown was (and is) the largest Chinese settlement in California, Chinese have lived and worked in all parts of the state. In the fertile Sacramento Delta, the Chinese town of Locke has attracted attention for over half a century. But the story of its inhabitants has never been told. This book is intended to remedy that situation.

The people of Locke form part of the last wave of immigrants from China to have come to California during the period of Oriental restriction and exclusion. How they managed to emigrate, what they experienced in California in the early part of this century, and how they later adapted to this country as citizens are an important part of the history of the Sacramento River Delta. As the Sacramento Delta, in turn, transmits its agricultural riches to us, we find that the people of Locke have an influence far beyond the boundaries of their town. In addition, their stories are interesting.

Locke is the last remaining Chinese town in the United States. However, it is fast disappearing. The town as a whole is shrinking, and in addition, non-Chinese have recently begun to live there. In 1970 there were only 150 Chinese residents in Locke. By 1976, that had shrunk to sixty-four and by 1980, to forty-two including eighteen first-generation, eleven second-generation, and thirteen third-generation Chinese.

To learn something of the town and its people before it disappeared altogether, my assistant and I began interviewing the residents in the summer of 1979. The following summer I conducted further interviews by myself. During these two summers, some twenty people were interviewed, all of them over sixty-five years of age and long-time residents of the town. Two of the people were women, and eighteen were men. All but one of those people were born in China, and the interviewing had to be done in Cantonese.

In the summer of 1981 I conducted more interviews. For further information and clarification, several people who lived outside Locke in places such as Courtland, Walnut Grove and Sacramento were interviewed. This time, in addition to Chinese immigrants, I also approached American farmers, Chinese American farmers, and several merchants and other residents who have been in the Delta long enough to know its early history. By the time I finished, I had interviewed about fifty people. The length of each interview varied between two and fifteen hours. Some people were interviewed in one session; others in five or even ten sessions. In several instances these stories have been difficult to glean from the individual. Some persons were reluctant to discuss their past, displaying diffidence or even suspicion when questioned about their early years.

PETER C.Y. LEUNG

Asian American Studies
University of California, Davis
May, 1984

Acknowledgements

This book is based on research I conducted between 1979 and 1982. My research was made possible by a grant from the Agricultural Experiment Station of the University of California at Davis and a Summer Faculty Research Development award from the Vice-Chancellor for Academic Affairs at the same institution. I wish to express my gratitude to the University for this support, and also to Professor Marc Pilisuk of the Department of Applied Behavioral Sciences, whose interest in my project was essential for its completion. I also thank the Stanford Area Chinese Club for their support when I was preparing the photographs and graphic work. It is my honor to have received endorsements from the California Secretary of State March Fong Eu and Senate Majority Leader Garamendi (see p. 83).

Professor David Brody of Davis' History Department read an early draft of the manuscript and provided helpful comments. The draft manuscript was also carefully and thoroughly edited and reworked by Dr. L. Eve Armentrout Ma, an historian who specializes in Chinese and Chinese American history. She is primarily responsible for researching and writing chapter four, "Locke, California," and contributed to chapter five, "Daily Life of the Delta's Chinese Farm Laborers and Tenant Farmers." Any errors elsewhere in the book are, of course, my own.

Without the participation of many residents of the Locke community, and people in the Delta and Sacramento area, it would have been impossible to document the experiences and the history of Chinese in the Delta. My special acknowledgements go to Wong Yow, So Yung Ng, Alfred Jung, Jack Chew, Steven Chan, Joy Low, Henry Wong, Tommy King, Ping Lee, Lincoln Chan, Hoi Kee, Sam Sun, Bob Sune, Po Jang, Joe Young, Choi Sun and his daughter Mrs. Chan, Mrs. Jong Ho Leong, Mrs. Joe Chow, George Adams, Joe Green, Jr., Mr. and Mrs. Edward Dutra, Bob Jang, and George Fong. I wish also to thank Stella Wong, Fred Li, and Esther Sanematsu who assisted with the interviews, as well as with the translation and organizing of the material. I am also grateful for the clerical support provided by the staff in the Department of Applied Behavioral Sciences. Finally, I wish to thank my wife, Eileen, without whose encouragement and pertinent criticisms this book would never have become a reality.

Peter C.Y. Leung
University of California, Davis
May, 1984

Introduction

The Sacramento Delta is considered one of the wonders of California. More than 750 square miles in area, it consists of a group of essentially manmade (or "man enlarged") islands and more than one thousand five hundred miles of scenic waterways. Once thousands of Miwok, Maidu and other Indians lived in the Delta's marshland. In the eighteenth century, Spanish missionaries and pioneers began to settle in California and after 1827, Americans joined them, some taking up residence on the Delta's islands where they raised wheat and cattle. With the discovery of gold at Coloma in 1848, shortly after the United States had annexed California, the Delta became a gateway to the foothills through which miners reached the mining camps by traveling along the Sacramento and San Joaquin Rivers.

By the 1850s, many people came to realize that the Delta held great potential for agricultural development. The swampy land and incessant flooding of the region made it obvious that extensive reclamation work was in order. The California State Legislature passed the Swamp and Overflow Act of 1861 to encourage levee building for reclamation purposes. Subsequently, Chinese laborers under contract to American developers built hundreds of miles of levees. Their task was arduous, requiring them to work in waist-deep water in an area in which malaria was still endemic. They cut drainage ditches, built floodgates, and slowly piled up small levees. In this fashion, between 1860 and 1880 a total of 88,000 acres was reclaimed from the Delta marshlands. Although these "China Levees" were later rebuilt with modern equipment, they were the foundation for today's levee network and for Delta agribusiness.

Once the land finally became fit for agriculture, the Chinese remained in the Delta to plant, maintain, harvest and preserve the crops that the land supported. Thousands of them worked in this capacity throughout the 1870s, both as agricultural laborers and as tenant farmers. When in 1882 the United States instituted the Chinese Exclusion Act and other legislation designed to prevent further immigration of Chinese laborers to the United States, the number of Chinese in the Delta began to decline. Chinese made a partial comeback in the 1920s and 1930s, but since the onset of World War II their numbers have steadily decreased to the point that today, there are probably fewer than ten Chinese farmers active in the Delta. However, their labor helped turn the Delta's extremely fertile, organic soil into a major agricultural area and secure California's position as a world leader in agricultural production.

In addition to its agricultural importance, the Delta is a naturally beautiful, estuarian environment which provides endless variety for outdoor activities. Whether

your hobby is boating, camping, birdwatching, fishing, picnicing or just browsing through quaint little towns, it can be enjoyed in the Delta. The most popular recreational activities are fishing and boating. Catfish and striped bass, sturgeon, salmon and steelhead can all be taken. Beaches, boating docks and other waterside facilities are numerous in the region. It is no surprise that every year, several million people come from every part of California to use the Delta's facilities.

The Sacramento Delta is rich in historical and scenic spots. Highway 160 follows the meanderings of the Sacramento River. Leaving Sacramento, the traveler comes first to the 120 year old, ramshackled community of Freeport, a town just beyond the limits of urban development. Soon, however, the city will reach out and swallow it, for the town as well as the thousands of acres of surrounding farmland are slated to be replaced by residential and commercial buildings. Quite naturally, the local farmers, most of whose ancestors started working this land in the 1880s, are very unhappy about the coming development.

Continuing the journey down Highway 160, the second town that the traveler encounters is Hood. Established in 1909, it was named after William Hood, chief construction engineer for the Southern Pacific Railway Company. Hood currently has a population of about 500. In addition, the surrounding pear orchards contain beautiful Victorian ranch houses. The traveler is struck by the grandeur of these houses, built nearly a century ago by pioneer farmers in the Delta. The traveler will also notice numerous run-down sheds and huts which once housed the area's farm laborers.

Continuing down Highway 160 the traveler has the Sacramento River on his right, while on the left, acres of farmland are cultivated alternately with pear trees and field crops. During the winter, one might see two or three laborers standing at the top of a ladder pruning trees. Sometimes, a yellowish fume rises into the sky around some of the orchards: this is the fumigation of the trees. During the winter, all the pear trees are naked with the trunks and branches perfectly bare. Some trees have been pruned and one can admire the skill of the workmen who did the job; other trees still have tangled branches waiting for the pruner's shears to prepare them for the coming new year's growth. During the spring, miles and miles of glorious pear blossoms smile at the blue sky, inviting the bees to visit. The crop fields begin to wear a new green clothing. When summer comes, thousands of pears hang down among the green leaves. Acres of corn fields and vegetable crops cover land not given over to pears.

Every year in July, an annual Pear Fair is celebrated at Courtland, the next town beyond Hood. The Delta is the most important pear producing area in the United States, and yields thirty percent of California's pear crop. It is also the earliest pear producing region in the United States. There are over 6,000 acres of pears in the Delta, producing an average of 100,000 tons each year. Delta acreage averages thirteen

to fourteen tons per unit while the statewide average is only nine to ten tons per acre.

Courtland's Pear Fair is held on the former high school grounds. This tiny Delta community devotes much of its energy to the annual preparations. The day-long fair features musical entertainment, food, contests, pears of numerous different varieties, a pear peeling competition, the big pear weigh-in, pear packing demonstrations and pear canning competitions.

Before leaving Courtland, the beauty of the former Bank of Courtland's building will definitely catch your eye. This building was erected in 1920. It is a handsome structure, one of the most imposing in any town in the Delta. In addition, the Bank of Courtland was a great factor in the advancement of the Delta's farming industry.

Having passed Courtland, the river once again demands attention. This is often a busy part of the river where high speed water ski boats create white waves. Luxurious yachts carrying tourists float by, while their passengers enjoy the peace and beauty of the Delta scenery. In the old days, the Sacramento River was an important transportation link, joining San Francisco Bay to the heart of California. Steamers like the *Chrysopolis, Nevada, Yosemite, Washoe,* and *Capitol* represented the ultimate in river transportation in the 1860s. Unfortunately, disasters often struck these steamers because their boilers exploded. For example, on October 12, 1865, the steamer *Yosemite* caught fire just as it left Rio Vista. There was an explosion and bodies hurled through the air, landing in the river and on the wharf. About eighty passengers died including every Chinese person on board.

In spite of disasters, however, steamers brought people and fruit (even then a big Delta crop) up and down the river, from Sacramento to San Francisco and all the river towns in between. Steamers played an important role in the development of the Delta's agriculture. The *Delta King* and *Delta Queen* were the two largest, most luxurious and most famous. Built partly in Scotland, they were completed in Stockton, California in 1926. They were each 285 feet long, weighed 1,837 tons gross and had 2,000 pound engines. Each steamer could accommodate 238 passengers and 2,000 tons of cargo. The *Delta King* and *Delta Queen* would leave San Francisco at six in the evening, and arrive in Sacramento at five thirty the next morning. In the 1920s a round trip cost one dollar fifty cents. Both steamers were taken out of public service in 1941.

After Courtland the next town the traveler encounters is Locke, a tiny community of perhaps seventy people, the last Chinese town in North America and the focus of this book. With its single paved street and aging buildings, its few Chinese signs and unique history, it has become an important stop for weekend tour buses whose passengers threaten to outnumber the town's inhabitants. Just across the slough from Locke is the town of Walnut Grove. With its five or six restaurants, several hundred

inhabitants and tiny Chinese and Japanese section, it resembles most of the other river towns. Behind and on the sides of the town stretch pear orchards; in front sits a large, steel drawbridge over which Highway 160 now runs, only to follow the river again along the top of the opposite levee. Some ten miles further on, the traveler arrives at the last and largest Delta town: Rio Vista (where the *Yosemite* blew up). Rio Vista lies at a crossroads, with one highway leading into California's Central Valley, the other working its way to the San Francisco Bay Area where the traveler will find himself out of the Delta, and back in "civilization."

The romance, the beauty and the productivity of the Delta all depend in the final analysis on the river's being brought under control. Next, they depend upon skillful farmers (including those with the ability to invest and manage the huge ranches, and those who actually worked in the orchards and fields). On both counts, we're reminded of the Chinese who built the first levees and planted the first crops. Once so numerous in the area, Chinese are now only occasionally in evidence. The once flourishing Chinatowns and Chinese villages have shrunk almost to the point of disappearing but their legacy lives on. In an attempt to recapture something of this past, I went to the last remaining Chinese town in the Delta, the tiny community of Locke. Through the townspeople and through others in the Delta, I have tried to reconstruct the Chinese side of the Delta's history, and keep North America's last remaining Chinese village from passing unnoticed into oblivion.

Part I: Locke, and the Delta's Chinese

Chapter 1

The Story of Chinese Immigration

According to ancient Chinese accounts, seafaring explorers from the Celestial Realm may have landed on America's west coast as early as the fifth century A.D. However, the modern history of Chinese in California does not begin until the mid-nineteenth century. One source claims that a few arrived in 1848 or 1849, having come via Peru (in which country attempts were being made to enslave them). Another account places the initial arrival of Chinese in California as taking place on February 2, 1848, when a certain Charles V. Gillespie landed in San Francisco with one woman and two men he had brought from China on the brig *Eagle*. And an article from the *San Francisco Star* dated April 1, 1848, mentions the presence of "two or three 'Celestials' in the city," while U.S. government accounts claim there were about fifty Chinese in the whole of California.

When news of the discovery of gold at Sutter's Mill reached San Francisco late in 1848, the Gold Rush was on. At just about the same time, the trickle of Chinese immigration turned into a flood, and Chinese joined others in the stampede to the gold fields. In the year 1851 alone, some 2,719 Chinese entered California (while between 1820 and 1850, the total was probably under 100).

The Chinese who began streaming into California in 1850-1851 were primarily unmarried men voluntarily emigrating from the southern, coastal provice of Kwangtung. Most came as sojourners, hoping to stay only long enough to reap a fortune, then return to their homes in China. Their families were often very poor and there was neither sufficient farm land nor jobs enough (in the cities as in the countryside) to support all of them. In addition to the need to sustain themselves, geographical as well as social and political elements inspired their journeys.

At this time, China pursued what has been called the "closed door policy." Among other things, this meant that the ruling Ch'ing Dynasty forbade emigration, viewing those who left as criminals to be beheaded upon their return. China's social, religious, and intellectual tradition also discouraged foreign travel. Furthermore, China felt it had no use for "barbarians" from the West and contact between Chinese and Western traders was discouraged (although by 1900, many Western traders had begun smuggling opium into South China on a large scale). Before 1840, only one port in the entire country was open for trade with the West: Canton located in Kwangtung

province. But because it did receive the Western traders, the people from the Canton area were somewhat acquainted with what was happening in Europe and America. And, when news of the gold discovery in California reached them, poverty made the gold sound very inviting.

Internal circumstances did as much to "push" the Chinese to California as the lure of gold "pulled" them. From about 1840 to 1870, China suffered a series of natural and political disasters which impoverished the country as a whole. The disasters also produced the seeds of rebellion which eventually culminated in the overthrow of the Manchu Ch'ing Dynasty in 1911. The natural disasters to which I refer were significant overpopulation, periodic floods and droughts, and resultant famines.

The political disasters included the decline of the Manchus. A series of rather inept, sometimes corrupt rulers had failed to keep the country strong, with the partial result that in 1842 China lost the Opium War with England, and the Arrow War with England and France in 1856. As a consequence of these two defeats, more of China was opened to Western trade. Opium smuggling became widespread, and Western goods began to drive out some native industries. A serious silver drain developed, causing severe inflation (since the country was on a silver standard). War reparations to England and France forced a major increase in taxes, further impoverishing the peasants. In 1851, partly as a result of these factors, the Taiping Rebellion against the Imperial government broke out. During the same period, there were uprisings in the Pearl River Delta of Kwangtung province, and feuds between two parts of the populace in that same area. These devastated the land and frustrated efforts to grow food. Consequently, emigration to California's "Mountain of Gold" seemed to some an ideal solution.

Although many wanted to travel to California, few could afford the passage. Some borrowed the fare from members of their own families. Others accepted the terms of emigration companies, whereby their fare was paid and they were to work for a certain number of months or years in the new land to repay the debt (after which their obligation came to an end). It was through these companies and this "credit-ticket" system that the Central Pacific Railroad in 1866 began recruiting laborers for its construction crews in California.

The first wave of Chinese immigrants streamed in to the gold mines, but the mines began to decline in productivity after the late 1850s. The second wave of Chinese was recruited by the Central Pacific Railroad when it could not find enough white, Mexican, or other migratory laborers to build the western section of the transcontinental railroad. The Chinese crews distinguished themselves by their industry and capability to learn quickly, despite the language barrier. The railroad was completed in 1869. With respect to California's population as a whole, after the decline of the gold mines and the completion of the transcontinental railroad, there was a demographic shift

4

from the mountains to cities and farmlands, and an economic shift from mining and the railroad to manufacturing and agriculture.

In San Francisco, unemployed Chinese released from railroad work found jobs in services such as laundries, garment production, cigar making, shoe manufacture, and restaurants, to name but a few. Some who settled in Sonoma and Napa Counties were instrumental in developing the vineyards. To the south in Orange County, the Chinese knowledge of agriculture was vital to the planting of vast orange groves. Those who settled in the Sacramento River Delta were employed in land reclamation and agricultural work.

The confluence of the Sacramento and San Joaquin Rivers runs through extremely fertile land. A system of smaller tributaries (sloughs) feeds the two rivers, forming a series of islands in the area. Until the middle of the nineteenth century, annual flooding prevented this desirable region from being utilized as farmland. However, it is popularly reported that Reuben Kercheval on Grand Island began to build levees against the Sacramento River in 1852: the first person to do so. Since horses and mules were too heavy to transport construction materials over the delicate peat, Kercheval used Chinese, Kanakas, and Indians. The first levees were periodically destroyed by floods. It was not until the 1870s that improved techniques permitted the land to be reclaimed with more permanent success. Again, the Chinese formed a vital part of the labor force on the construction of these newer levees.

When the land finally was fit for agriculture, the Chinese remained to plant, maintain, harvest and preserve the crops that the land supported. Although most studies indicate that grain was originally the primary crop, by the mid-1870s it became apparent that fruit orchards and certain vegetables were financially more rewarding. Soon afterwards, canneries arose near the orchards and farms to handle the produce as soon as it was harvested.

The Chinese laborers were industrious and efficient and learned each new job quickly. In general, they were neither carousers nor idlers. Their goal helps to explain this. Most wanted to earn money in California so as to return to China rich enough to buy some land to add to the family possessions, and retire to a life of leisure. Some actually succeeded in doing this, but for the majority the sojourn turned into years— often, the better part of a lifetime. In the meantime, they sent much of their pay to their families in China to help support parents, wives and children, aunts and uncles, brothers and sisters and anyone else who might live in the family unit. The laborer kept only enough for room and board and possibly a little for entertainment. Most of these Chinese pioneers had no intention of settling in America, and they felt little need to become fluent in English or adopt American customs. They sought each other's company to stave off loneliness and preserved Chinese customs to help remind them of home.

Although they did not intend their stay to become permanent, they were nevertheless interested in other Californians and the "foreign customs" they observed. A few Chinese did, of course, learn English, often acting as interpreters for their fellow countrymen. Some adopted Western dress and became Americanized. A much larger number, while remaining more obviously "Chinese," still desired to participate in a positive way in the New World in which they found themselves.

Originally, this Chinese amity was reciprocated by Americans. In San Francisco they were invited to be one of the major celebrants at the funeral procession of President Zachery Taylor, and to help celebrate various national holidays. In the railroad camps their importance was acknowledged. Even if they seemed strange to other miners, at first the latter did not chase the Chinese off of claims, especially since Chinese often mined areas already abandoned by white gold hunters. This tolerant attitude did not last long, however. When gold began to be less plentiful after the mid-1850s American miners, supported by the Northern European immigrants, grew to resent any dark-skinned "interlopers," including the Chinese. Many attempts were made to preserve California for white Americans.

In the next two decades resentment turned to violent hostility as California underwent a series of disturbing changes. The Civil War had adversely affected Eastern industries with the result that at first, infant California businesses were able to compete successfully. This created jobs, but due to a manpower shortage, wages in California were much higher than anywhere else in the country. With the end of the Civil War and, more importantly, the completion of the transcontinental railroad, the situation changed dramatically. Eastern industries resumed operations, threatening to bankrupt the new Pacific Coast companies. The railroad daily brought more adventurers to the land of sunshine, eager to reap the easy wealth of which they had heard; and this created a surfeit of available unskilled labor. Finally, the depression which hit the Eastern states in the late 1860s reached California by the early 1870s. The Chinese, conspicuously different and laboring for wages that were considered cheap by California's standards (although they were high compared to those of the East Coast), were made scapegoats and held responsible for most of California's problems.

In a series of laws, California attempted to eliminate what it considered the "Yellow Peril." California's Foreign Miner's Tax of 1855 was levied mainly against Mexicans and Chinese. In the same year, the Chinese Passenger Tax sought to keep Chinese out of the state entirely. These two laws were followed by a state exclusion act in 1858, a white labor protection act in 1862, and other discriminatory legislation. Although most of these laws were declared unconstitutional by the courts, they made the rest of the country aware of the depth of anti-Chinese sentiment in California. National political concerns of the post-Civil War era made the federal government anxious to placate Californians.

6

In 1868 the Burlingame Treaty established reciprocal privileges between the United States and China with respect to immigrants, as well as dealing with other matters. However, the Treaty of 1880 modified this pact, allowing immigration limits to be set solely by the United States; and the Chinese Exclusion Laws of 1882 suspended most new Chinese immigration for a period of ten years and denied Chinese the right of naturalization. The Scott Act of 1888 further limited Chinese immigration and made it difficult for Chinese already living in the United States to leave this country and then return. In 1892, the Geary Act extended the Chinese Exclusion Act for another ten years, and in 1902, exclusion was made a permanent condition. This law was not repealed until 1943 (the same year in which Chinese regained the right of naturalization). Even after 1943, however, only a very few Chinese were allowed to enter each year. Not until 1965 was Chinese immigration put on the same footing as immigration from the rest of the world.

Discriminatory legislation was not enough to satisfy the anti-Chinese forces, especially the members of Denis Kearney's Workingman's Party. By the 1860s Chinese disembarking from the ships docked in San Francisco were pelted with rocks and jeered by mobs of white hoodlums. Numerous acts of violence occurred in the mining camps. In small cities and towns, the local Chinatowns might be torched, or their residents escorted out of town at gun point. In cities as far apart as Los Angeles and Rock Springs, Wyoming, major riots resulted in many Chinese killed by whites. As a result of the violence and the discriminatory legislation, the number of Chinese to immigrate to the United States went from a high of 123,000 in the period 1860-1870, to only 15,000 two decades later. After 1900, their numbers declined even more sharply. Until President Johnson removed their quota in 1965, the flow of Chinese immigrants into the United States remained a trickle.

The primary intent of the Exclusion Laws was to prevent Chinese laborers from entering the United States. Teacher, students, merchants, and tourists were still allowed to come. The wives of resident Chinese merchants and, for a while, the wives of native-born Chinese Americans were also granted entry; for most of this period the China-born children of resident Chinese were as well.

Furthermore, there were means of circumventing the Exclusion Laws. Quite a few Chinese gained entrance because they produced witnesses who testified that they were merchants. Something called the "slot system" also developed: a married man returning to visit his wife in China might stay several months, long enough to father a child. Upon returning to America he would then declare that he had begotten a child, even if in fact no child had been born. If his wife had given him a daughter, the man might declare it was a son. In either case, fifteen or twenty years later he could sell the "slot" of his fictitious son to some young man in China whose family wanted him to immigrate to the United States. For the hopeful immigrants, known as "paper sons," it was

expensive, but anxious to better their condition, many entered the country in this manner during the years of strictest exclusion. San Francisco's earthquake and fire in 1906 helped this enterprise since all the records of immigrants and their status were destroyed. It was harder for American officials to determine who was a *bona fide* son and who was a "paper son".

California's port of entry for all Chinese between 1910 and 1940 was Angel Island in San Francisco Bay. There, a detention station was built where incoming Chinese were segregated from other races and nationalities. (Men were housed separately from women.) Although other immigrants were processed fairly rapidly, the Chinese were kept for weeks, sometimes months, while their papers were checked and rechecked and their stories told again and again to officials. It was a frightening and sometimes humiliating experience. Angel Island was finally closed in 1940 on the grounds that it was unsanitary and unfit for habitation. The memory of what they went through left a permanent blot on the memories of most Chinese immigrants of this time.

These conditions formed the prevailing atmosphere when the Chinese immigrated to the Sacramento Delta. Either they came legally as legitimate children or wives of resident Chinese, or they entered by means of purchased "slots." They settled in areas where others of their families or from the same district in China had already settled. The two major districts represented in the Delta were the Sze Yup and Chungshan districts (both located near Canton). Chinese from these two districts felt a great deal of animosity towards each other; animosity which has been kept alive in the United States. The town of Locke has always been a Chungshan town, so we shall now have a look a Chungshan County.

Chapter 2

The Old Home in South China's Chungshan County

Kwangtung, a province situated in southeastern China, is a coastal province and an important one. Its capital, Canton, lies to the south on the Pearl River almost at the mouth of the Pearl River estuary at a point eighty miles from the South China Sea. The province as a whole encompasses 90,247 square miles and has a population of 42,800,000. The northern counties are mountainous and hilly, with relatively few inhabitants. The southern part of the province, however, contains the densely populated flatlands of the Pearl River Delta. Located near the equator, Kwangtung enjoys a warm climate with an average temperature of 72° F throughout the year. Its summer lasts seven to eight months. The warm climate, abundance of water and rich soil found in the lowlands make Kwangtung Province, and especially the Pearl River Delta, an ideal agricultural area. About twenty percent of Kwangtung is farmland, most of which is located in the Pearl River Delta and the Chiuh Saan Plain (on the southeast coastal region of Kwangtung). Because of the long growing season, each field can normally produce several crops a year.

The Pearl River is Kwangtung's largest river, formed from the confluence of the East River, West River, and North River. The delta comprises about five percent of the entire province and is about the size of Hawaii Island. In spite of its size, it accounts for almost half of the agricultural production of the entire province. The chief crops are sugar cane, paddy rice, silkworms and mulberries with large tracts also given over to orchards and fish ponds. The delta itself is geographically unusual, for it contains hills as well as flatlands. These hills, or high spots, were originally islands along the bay. Silt deposits from the river slowly joined them to the mainland, a process that even now is reaching out to other islands. Almost the entire delta has been put to the plow with the exception of land occupied by cities, towns, the numerous farming and fishing villages, and a few industrial sites. Most of the industry is crop-related. The factories weave silk, process sugar, and produce farm chemicals and construction materials. Because of its dense network of waterways, the delta is also Kwangtung's center of water transportation along which fruit, sugar, sugar cane, cattle, fish, salt, timber, cloth and the like are transported.

For the past several hundred years, the Pearl River Delta has been divided into seven counties of which Chungshan County is the richest. A hilly area, it borders both the ocean and the bay. The county's original name was Heungshan, or "Fragrant Moun-

tain" because of the profusion of wild, flowering plants that used to thrive in the area. The flowers' fragrance was said to be so strong that it could be detected ten miles away. In 1925 the name was formally changed to Chungshan to commemorate the death of the great revolutionary hero and the first President of China, Dr. Sun Yat-sen (since Chungshan was one of Dr. Sun's many names).

The 1,033 square miles which make up the county may be divided into three geographical areas. The middle of the county is mountainous, while there are flatlands in the north, and islands along the county's southern edge. The flatlands are laced with waterways which spread out and recombine, forming an intricate network which controls all the water for agriculture and water transportation. Through these waterways, the county links the inland regions with the sea. It is strategically situated between several large cities and the international port of Canton. Even closer than Canton, the Portuguese outpost of Macao and the great free port of Hong Kong give Chungshan County, and the whole of Kwangtung province, a window on the non-Chinese world as well as an even larger international market.

Canton

The ancient city of Canton, situated near the mouth of the Pearl River, is the capital of Kwangtung province and the biggest city in southern China (excluding Hong Kong, which is currently a British Colony). For centuries a major trade center, it was not until the sixteenth and seventeenth centuries that Westerners began to call regularly at Canton. In 1684 the British East India Company established an outpost there and secured a virtual monopoly of foreign trade, which it maintained until 1834. From 1757 until 1840, Canton was the only Chinese port where foreign trade could be legally carried on. Its major exports included silk, tea and fine porcelain; the principal imports were opium, cotton and textiles. After about 1840, imports greatly outdistanced exports.

Canton is a beautiful and fascinating city. Taken together with its suburbs, it houses more than 125 temples. The five-storied Pagoda and the spires of the Roman Catholic cathedral can be seen rising above the city as you approach by steamer. The city is famous for its old curios and bronzes, its ivory carvings, its embroiderries, silverware, blackwood furniture, screens, procelains and wonderful carved jade. Densely populated, Canton contained over three million people in 1975. Although the surrounding countryside is a rich agricultural area, it cannot produce enough to sustain this population and food has to be imported.

An important effect of the foreign trade was (until limited by the Communists in 1949) to encourage the emigration of Cantonese overseas. In fact, over half of all Chinese who went overseas came from Canton and its hinterland. Most emigrants went abroad because they were poor and wanted to earn money to bring back for

themselves and their families in China. Even though this emigration was illegal for most of the period between the seventeenth and the twentieth centuries, it was widespread and led to the growth of important Chinese enclaves throughout Southeast Asia, in North America, and elsewhere.

Hong Kong and Macao

Hong Kong, a British colony and one of the world's leading trade and international centers, is located some ninety miles from Canton and forty miles from the tiny Portuguese colony of Macao. With a total area of about 400 square miles, Hong Kong consists of Hong Kong Island, Kowloon, the New Territories and some 236 islands, all lying in the mouth of the Pearl River. About 150 years ago, before the arrival of the British, Hong Kong and Kowloon were no more than small fishing settlements. Hong Kong Island was ceded to Britain by China in 1842, after the Opium War. Britain acquired the rest of the territory between 1842 and 1898. It is Britain's last Asian colony. The New Territories leased from China (not ceded) for a period of 99 years are due to be returned in 1997. In part due to differing systems of government the exact fate of Hong Kong (ceded as well as leased territory) is unclear at this time although Great Britain and the People's Republic of China are currently trying to settle the question by negotiations.

During the later half of the 19th century and the early 20th century, Hong Kong developed into a great international trading port. The population rose from 33,000 in 1851 to 2.5 million in 1950, to over 5 million today. Important in its growth has been the influx of refugees, both from natural disasters and from political troubles. A large proportion of Hong Kong's present day inhabitants are people who fled the Chinese Communists. Because of its steadily mushrooming population and because many of the refugees during the period 1949-1952 brought with them industrial expertise, in recent decades Hong Kong has embarked on an industrial revolution. Hong Kong has also attracted foreign capital and industry, and large numbers of foreign tourists. Finally, since 1960 Hong Kong became the third most important financial market in the world (after London and New York).

Macao, like Rome, was built on seven hills. It is located on the southern coast of China, and it was founded in 1557 during an era of Portuguese exploration. With a total area of only six square miles, the colony comprises a peninsula, where the city of Macao is located, and the islands of Taipa and Coloane. At the extreme northern end of the penninsula there is a gateway at the border with China joining Macao to Chungshan County.

In the seventeenth century, Macao served as a vital base for merchants as well as for missionaries to China and Japan. Because of its prosperity and privileged location, other European nations coveted it and plotted to seize it from Portugal. When

the treaty ports were opened along the China coast and the British settled Hong Kong, the economic importance of Macao declined. Macao, however, continues to be important as a distribution outlet for rice, fish, piece goods and other Chinese products. The city has grown up with a strong Portuguese influence, evident in its classic Iberian churches, its cannon-studded fortresses, its winding cobblestone streets, and its public buildings and monuments. But it is also very much a Chinese city with a Chinese population of 261,000 people.

Chungshan County

The Pearl River Runs along Chungshan County's southeastern border. The land bordering the river is sandy. It contains tracts of rice land and other tracts which support mulberry trees and commercial fish ponds. Mulberries, silkworms, and fish ponds have developed into a single industry because each helps support the other: the leaves of the mulberry feed the silkworms, the mulberry roots hold the sandy soil in place so that fish ponds can be established in the lower sandy lots, the excrement of the silkworm is fed to the fish, and fish excrement fertilizes the mulberry. These form a very useful cycle in the agriculture of Chungshan. Other important crops in Chungshan County include bananas and lichee.

Around 1920 Chungshan County had about 87,000 people. The soil was so fertile, however, that the annual rice production was more than needed by its inhabitants. In addition, the county supplied most of the food for its neighboring counties, and even for the great city of Canton. Compared with its neighboring counties, Chungshan was not too poor. In spite of this, many people continued to emigrate overseas to earn a living and acquire an education. Yung Wing, who in 1854 became the first Chinese to graduate from Yale College, and Joe Shoong, a very successful merchant who founded the National Dollar Stores in California in the 1920s, were both natives of Chungshan.

Most of the immigrants from Chungshan, however, did not become either wealthy or famous and well-educated. Most of Locke's Chungshan inhabitants were either farm laborers or tenant farmers in the Sacramento Delta. Their situation in China prior to their arrival in the United States had usually been even more modest. As the long-time Locke resident, So Yung Ng explained,

> I was born in Dung Village, Chungshan County in China. When I was in my teens, I worked in my uncle's orchard. He grew many kinds of fruit, such as peaches, plums, lichees, loquats and tangerines. It was very difficult to make a living during those days in China. There was not enough food and few jobs and I only got ten cents for a whole day's work as a farm laborer. Nonetheless, I was considered lucky just to have been hired by a relative. Because of the poor economic conditions many people decid-

ed to leave their home country, China, and to go abroad to make a living rather than to remain in poverty at home.

Po Jang, who came to America in 1918 and settled in Locke tells us:

I was born at Houh Tauh Village, Chungshan County, China. I went to school for two years from age ten to twelve. I started working at odd jobs to earn money. I first went around to each house to collect eggs for a store which exported them to Hong Kong. Later, I worked as a laborer for a rickshaw company, carrying people in and out from the village to town. This job was hard and required a lot of strength but at that time I was young. I did not work for long at that job. I just tried to do something to make a living. In 1918 I borrowed money from my relatives and decided to go to America.

Mrs. Joe Chow adds:

Before I got married in China, my grandmother would not allow me or other girls to go to school. She argued that it was useless for girls to go to school. Instead I learned how to cook and to work in the rice fields. I came to the United States in the 1930s because the China-Japan War had broken out in China. At that time my husband was a farmer in the Sacramento Delta.

Chapter 3

Chinatowns in the Sacramento Delta

The Sacramento River Delta is the fertile bottom land around the Sacramento and San Joaquin Rivers. If one were to draw straight lines connecting the cities of Antioch, Tracy, Stockton, and Sacramento, the circumscribed region would approximate the Delta. It is one of the more important agricultural regions of California, a state in which agriculture is the number one industry. Farms, orchards, and ranches dominate the Delta. Most land is held in vast tracts of hundreds or even thousands of acres. Principal crops include potatoes, wheat, pears, and tomatoes. In addition to the farmland, the Delta contains a number of small to medium-sized towns, most dating from the 1850s, 1860s, and 1870s.

Chinese have been in the Delta at least since the 1860s. Most came from two adjoining areas of the Pearl River Delta: the Sze Yap (Four Counties) region, and Chungshan County. Those from Chungshan County have been the most numerous. The Chinese in the Delta have followed a number of occupations. Some have been merchants, others have been barbers, launderers, restaurant owners, labor contractors, or the like. The vast majority, however, have been farm laborers or tenant farmers or, in the early period (1860s and 1870s), levee builders.

The building of levees was necessary in order to reclaim the Delta's extremely fertile land for farming purposes. In the early decades, the work was done manually, but by the turn of the century, machines had begun to replace men as levee-builders. The machine-built levees were not only more rapidly constructed, they also were stronger and more permanent. Chinese laborers by the thousands formed the backbone of the early manual labor force, particularly up until 1882 when the first Chinese Exclusion Laws began to cut into their numbers.

Some of the earliest efforts at levee-building and reclamation used Chinese as part of the labor force. However, the main contingent of Chinese levee builders did not arrive until 1868 when newly-passed legislation encouraged the formation of reclamation districts, and reclamation began in earnest. At about the same time, the completion of the first transcontinental railroad released thousands of Chinese into the work force. Anxious for a job, they were more than willing to hire themselves out for work on the levee.

A system of labor which had already been systematized by the Chinese who worked on the railroad was put into effect on the levees. Land developers would contract with one English-speaking Chinese for a certain amount of levee to be built. This man,

15

as foreman and interpreter, would gather a crew of Chinese laborers whom he told when and where to work or rest; he also translated into Chinese any orders given him by his employer. Besides foreman and workmen and crew usually had its own cook. The gangs lived on the site in tents in order to waste no time. Crews varied in size according to the size of the job; there are instances of crews of eight as well as crews of thirty. The levees were made by constructing two pyramidal walls of sun dried tule bricks parallel to each other. The intervening space was filled with sandy mud. Horses were sometimes used to help level the levee tops. With few exceptions, these "China levees" were small and not totally impervious to the perennial innundations. They only provided a temporary solution to the problem of flooding.

Levee construction was hard work. In an effort to maximize the effects of the labor, innovations had to be developed. The Chinese were the first to devise the tule shoe, an oversized horseshoe originally made of ashboard and wired to the hooves of the horses used for leveling. This shoe distributed the animal's weight over a large area and prevented it from sinking into the soft peat. Recovery of land proceeded more quickly and efficiently after this. From 1860 to 1880, manual laborers — most of them Chinese — reclaimed approximately 88,000 acres of rich Delta land.

The payment for services rendered was quite cheap considering the vast area of land recovered. Originally working on a wage system, some Chinese foremen soon began to contract for payment of 13^c to $13\frac{1}{2}^c$ per cubic yard of land moved. Another system was to pay the foreman $1 a day for each laborer. The foreman would keep 10^c or 15^c of this, and pass the rest along to the laborer. To give an idea of the numbers involved, one ledger from the Overflowed Land Reclamation District, Number 303, shows that for the period July 1, 1877 to December 31, 1878 (eighteen months), a total of $253,780.09 was paid for Chinese labor, with another $6,620.84 owed. This constitutes seventy-two percent of the total expenditures for that period, and suggests that at least 500 Chinese were working on that portion of the levees at that time.

I interviewed Edward and Linda Dutra who own and operate a museum in Rio Vista, as well as own a dredging company. The museum is full of memorabilia — photographs, old letters, minute books, legal documents, and artifacts — which record the history of dredging in the Delta and include a few extant accounts of Chinese levee workers. Mr. Dutra's father was the first member of his family to hire Chinese. Dutra reports that manual laborers moved approximately 32,000,000 yards of land in the Delta; 913,000,000 yards were eventually reclaimed on a permanent basis by the dredges. The Chinese shoveled dredged mud into wheelbarrows and dumped the loads off the end of a barge. They also finished the tops of the levees built by the dredges, a job now done by graders. One of the few surviving examples of a tule shoe has been loaned for display in the Dutra Museum.

A local farmer, "David Jones" (pseu.), said until 1918 there were still Chinese

helping to build the levees. He recalls that his father was the levee contractor responsible for building a section of the levee right in front of their ranch in Clarksburg. Jones' father supervised about eight Chinese laborers in his team. The Chinese went down to the riverbed, shoveled the mud and sediment into the wheelbarrow, and built up the levee. And Tom Chow King of Locke remembers that his mother said her father-in-law helped build the levee. King's mother said that it used to flood in Courtland, where she lived. When the alarm was sounded, everyone would go to help to repair the levee.

Many of these levee builders stayed on in the Delta to become farm laborers and the like. Many lived in the Delta's towns, usually in tiny Chinatowns where common language and anti-Chinese sentiment relegated them. The most important Delta towns to contain Chinese settlements all lie on or very near the Sacramento River. Five of them are particularly important. Proceeding upriver, they are as follows: Rio Vista, Isleton, Walnut Grove, Locke, and Courtland.

Rio Vista was founded in 1857. First called Brazos Del Rio, the town got its present name in 1862 after a flood wiped it out and the town was rebuilt on higher ground. The town boasted the largest asparagus cannery in the world between 1890 and the 1920s. By 1878, the town had its own Chinatown which consisted of six houses, beginning at the north end of Front Street. Chinatown's most prominent citizen at that time was a man by the name of Toy Joe. There was also a "Chinese American Cemetery" located just outside of town, but around the turn of the century, most of the bodies were exhumed and shipped back to China for burial. Currently, the cemetery contains the marker of only one Chinese, that of a woman who died in 1927.

Mr. Stewart, whose family has operated a funeral parlor in Rio Vista since 1892, recalls a time when Chinese funeral ceremonies were very splendid and included a parade through the town. The parade might include a whole roasted pig and figures made of paper, such as a house for the spirit of the departed to use in the afterlife. There would also be a musical band accompanying the parade toward the cemetery.

In the 1890s, with the introduction of asparagus as a cash crop, Rio Vista ended a long period of stagnation and began to grow both in size and wealth. The Chinese section shared in this prosperity. It became a focal point for seasonal Chinese farm and orchard workers on their days off. There was also a fairly large, permanent population of Chinese, consisting of potato farmers, and long-term farm workers (the latter, mostly people employed on the asparagus farms). Almost all of these people came from the Sze Yap region in China (specifically Toi Shan County). The failure of the asparagus fields between 1910 and 1920, however, made Rio Vista's Chinatown the first in the Delta to die. Currently, only one house remains of Rio Vista's original Chinatown, although a few Chinese still operate businesses or live in the area.

According to one writer, asparagus as a commercial crop delayed the urbanization of the Chinese in the Sacramento Delta by about fifty years. It affected the entire Delta but especially Isleton and Rio Vista. Isleton was founded by Josiah Pool, a veteran of the Mexican War, in 1874. The census report indicates that by 1880, Isleton had 1,680 residents. Of these, 880 (or fifty-two percent) were Chinese and the rest were Caucasian. The Chinese noted their occupations as farmers or farm laborers, with the exception of a few fishermen, servants, and merchants. Actually, even before Isleton was founded, Chinese had already begun leasing land from Mr. Pool for farming. They planted sweet potatoes, white beans, and other crops on forty-four acres. After the crops were sold, the Chinese tenants paid Mr. Pool $1,100.

Isleton's original Chinese district was situated on Jackson Slough on the southwest end of the town near Lothrop Tract. It contained thirty-five residents. There were six or seven households, four stores and a laundry. The Chinese community burned twice. The buildings were wooden and close together. A fire in December of 1915 completely razed the district. It was immediately rebuilt, however, and life continued much as it had been until the day after Memorial Day in 1926 when another fire burned the buildings to the ground. Reconstruction again took place; this time the buildings were of tin, brick, and asbestos to protect against future fires. Besides fire, the town has also had to tolerate substantial flooding, most recently in 1972 due to a break in the levee. However, a few Chinese businesses remain even today, in operation since thé early days of the community.

Mrs. Gee Chin, a native daughter and longtime resident of Isleton, was born there in 1911. Her grandfather came to the town after his match factory (located somewhere near the Sierras) was destroyed by fire. Her grandfather told her that in those days Chinese made matches by hand. Her grandfather and his partner started a general merchandise store in the old part of Chinatown in Isleton. This store and many other buildings were burned down in 1926. Then her grandfather went back to China to retire and never came back. Mrs. Chin's father came to the United States when he was a teenager. At first he worked as a cook in a lumber camp in the Sierras. Later he worked at his father's store and also opened a restaurant. After the fire in 1926, he rebuilt the store in the same location on Isleton's main street. In the 1920s, in addition to working in the asparagus fields, many Chinese worked in potato ranches around there. Her father supplied food to these potato farmers.

Mrs. Chin's parents did not have any sons. She was the third girl and was very close to her father. She often helped in her father's store, which she later inherited and currently owns. Now called the Isleton Bait Shop, the store will probably pass on to Mrs. Chin's son. The only other businesses in town which are still Chinese-owned are two restaurants across the street from her, and Lee's Sporting Goods.

18

As a child, Mrs. Chin attended the segregated Oriental School in Isleton from the first grade to eighth grade. In the first grade class there were more than ten pupils, but in the eighth grade there are only four students left (three Chinese and one Japanese). Besides attending the Oriental School, she also attended Isleton's Chinese school for two years in the late afternoons and evenings, where she was taught Chinese. She said she enjoyed this very much because she could speak Chinese with her friends and also learned Chinese to help her father in bookkeeping and sales.

Isleton's Chinese community was composed of both Chungshan and Sze Yap people. In spite of this division, the Chinese did not have many problems among themselves; the only quarrels might involve money. These usually could be resolved when the matters were brought to their friends, or to the local branch of the community organization called the Bing Kung Tong. Mrs. Chin's father was the president of Bing Kung Tong for many years. The principal function of the Bing Kung Tong was to provide protection to Chinese businesses in town. Some other activities were to organize social gatherings, the celebration of Chinese New Years and a Spring banquet.

From the 1920s to the late 1940s, Isleton was at its economic height. Besides Chinese, there were Japanese and Filipinos living in Chinatown or patronizing its establishments. In addition to the Bing Kung Tong, and to other Chinese businesses, Chinatown had four gambling houses. Mrs. Chin also remembers that the National Cannery was purchased by a Chinese called Thomas Foon Chew, who came from San Francisco. He was the second Chinese to operate a cannery by himself. Besides this cannery, other canneries also hired many Chinese workers, especially women workers.

Located seven miles upriver from Isleton, Walnut Grove was founded in 1851 by John W. Sharp. The town was extremely small until steamboats on the San Francisco-Sacramento run began to stop there in the 1870s. A stage line and bridges soon followed.

Chinese have been living in Walnut Grove probably since the day it was founded. Until the 1950s they made up a fairly large percentage of the town's population. In the early days, many must have been levee builders while others found jobs in the orchards and farms and, by the 1880s and 1890s, in the newly opened canneries. By this time if not sooner, Walnut Grove's Chinatown boasted restaurants, general stores, and other shops (some of which remain to this day.).

Like Isleton, up until World War II much of the town's Chinese population was transient, depending upon the agricultural cycle for its employment. Also like Isleton, most of these Chinese involved in agriculture worked in the orchards or on potato farms. In Walnut Grove, boarding houses run by Chinese for the Chinese laborers were numerous. In the 1920s, these charged an average of five dollars a month for a room with two beds and a place to cook. Farm workers on their day off and on

rainy days patronized Chinatown's gambling parlors and whorehouses, of which there were several in Walnut Grove especially up through Prohibition.

Walnut Grove's Chinatown burned to the ground at least two times, but was rebuilt after each fire. The first fire occurred in 1915. Prior to that date, the Chinese community had consisted of both Sze Yap and Chungshan people. These two groups of Chinese, even though from neighboring regions of the Pearl River Delta, spoke two different dialects of Chinese and often felt antagonistic towards each other in America as in China. This antagonism led the majority of Walnut Grove's Chungshan people to move out of town after the 1915 fire and found their own community, the little town of Locke, located just across the slough from Walnut Grove.

The second fire in Walnut Grove's Chinatown occurred in 1937. In the years between the two fires, the town's Chinese community had regained its former size by the influx of Chinese from Courtland. These latter had been evicted from Courtland in 1930 by a fire which had destroyed their Chinatown, and a landlord who refused to let them rebuild after the fire. (American laws made it almost impossible for Chinese to own land in California at that time.) After the late 1940s, however, the number of Chinese who sought work as agricultural laborers greatly diminished and Walnut Grove's Chinatown began a final decline. There are only a handful residing in the town at the present time, although one of the Delta's most successful Chinese American farming families (Lum Bunn Fong's Sons) lives within several miles of Walnut Grove.

Wong Yow, a retired farm laborer who currently lives in Locke recalls that when he first came to the Sacramento Delta in 1921, he lived with his father in Walnut Grove. They shared a room in a boarding house. When they were working, they had their meals at the ranch, but when they did not have work, they gathered dry wood and branches to use as fuel for cooking in the boarding house.

Although born in China, Ming Ma grew up in Walnut Grove and has operated a barber shop there for several decades. He learned his trade in Oakland, then he worked for four months in San Francisco. In 1929 he returned to Walnut Grove to start his own business. There were eight barbershops in town at the time, but he was the only Chinese barber. Approximately 800 Chinese were then living in Walnut Grove, but the population increased to over 1,000 during the harvest season. The whole town was crowded with people. His business and the other Chinese businesses were very prosperous at that time. He charged 50ᶜ for a haircut. During the busiest days, usually on weekends, he worked more than ten hours a day and could earn as much as $50 a day.

Ming Ma remembers the second fire to destroy Chinatown, the one which occurred in 1937. That fire broke out at 4:30 a.m. It burned down eighty houses: the

20

entire area from the railroad to the highway. It lasted more than four hours. While he talked to me, he pointed to many empty lots that have never been rebuilt. Two retired Chinese farm laborers were burned to death in a house directly in back of his shop. One of them was over sixty years old when he died.

Alfred Jung, currently a resident of Sacramento, recalls that one summer he worked in a Chinese-owned dry goods store in Walnut Grove. Besides taking care of the regular customers, the owner asked him to collect *pak-kop piu* tickets (Chinese keno, a form of lottery) at the store. The players were mostly farm workers and all were Chinese. At that time many Chinese stores sold the lottery tickets as a side business during the summer. The stores sold and collected the tickets, but the lottery itself was operated by the gambling houses. There were two games a day, and because regular stores could sell the tickets, people did not have to go to a gambling house in order to play the game.

Partly in order to regulate the gambling business, partly to regulate other businesses, and partly to manage general employer-employee relations (in cases where both were Chinese), the Bing Kung Tong established a branch in Walnut Grove during the 1910s or 1920s. This organization also performed important social functions: it helped indigent Chinese return to their native land, or sent the bones of the deceased back to the ancestral village for burial. It also hosted three big festivals each year with accompanying banquets and, in the 1930s, 1940s, and 1950s, a performance of Cantonese opera. The Bing Kung Tong also helped secure the repayment of debts and mediated most quarrels between members of the Chinese community. In a word, it was Chinatown's most important social organization, although not the only one. In the 1930s, there was also a Chinese Benevolent Association (Chung-wah wai-gun, or Chung-hua hui-kuan) which helped represent the Chinese community to Americans. For a time, it took over some of the "social service" duties of the Bing Kung Tong. By 1945, however, it had disappeared.

At its height, Walnut Grove's Bing Kung Tong boasted an active membership of some 400 men. Isleton and even Courtland have had to close the doors of their Bing Kung Tong branch for lack of sufficient members, but the branch in Walnut Grove is still viable. According to the recently deceased Bob Suen, several times president of the organization, in recent years the emphasis has been on the three yearly festivals (Chinese New Year's, the Spring banquet, and induction of officers) and on social activities such as golf tournaments. Its current, somewhat more social, character is partly due to the lack of businesses to regulate, partly to the decline in gambling, and partly to the shrunken size of the Delta's Chinese community.

Less than a mile from Walnut Grove, just across the slough, is the Chinese town of Locke which is the focus of this book. Since the whole of the following chapter will be devoted to Locke, however, I shall skip over it for the present. About ten miles beyond Locke lies the town of Courtland, the last in the series of old Delta towns

21

which I shall discuss. James V. Sims, a miner turned farmer, founded this sleepy little town in the 1860s. Once a booming community with several fish canneries, Courtland housed a large Chinese population. The presence of Chinese was due to the canneries and to the surrounding pear orchards. In fact, Courtland was the center of the Delta's fruit district.

At its height in the 1910s and 1920s, Courtland's Chinatown boasted over 500 people. Only one of the shops is still in existence today. The Chinatown was composed of fairly permanent residents, fruit workers and potato farmers from permanent crews, and tenant farmers. In December of 1879 some Chinese merchants were planning to open a garment factory in the town when their community burned. The settlement was rebuilt and remained active in spite of two more fires until 1930 when a fourth fire burned it down. This time the landowners refused to renew the lease. Most of the residents emmigrated to Locke and Walnut Grove.

In spite of the greatly reduced size of the Chinese community, those remaining behind rebuilt Chinatown at another location. Chief among those was Chong Chan, a shopkeeper and successful farmer who had lived in Walnut Grove since 1908. A man with community spirit as well as good business sense, he helped Chinatown rebuild after the 1930 fire just as he had after two earlier fires. In 1910 he had hosted the Chinese revolutionary leader Dr. Sun Yat-sen, and contributed very generously to his cause (a cause which achieved success the following year when the infant Republic of China was established with Dr. Sun as its first, provisional president). Again in 1937, Chong Chan, along with other of the Delta's Chinese, contributed toward the establishment in Walnut Grove of a Chinese Benevolent Association (Chung-wah wai-gun, or Chung-hua hui-kuan). This latter organization was founded in order to honor the visit to Courtland of a Chinese hero, General Tsai Teng Kai, who had recently distinguished himself in China's war with Japan. Finally, until the mid-1940s, Chong Chan hosted a Sunday dinner of chicken and rice for all the Chinese who lived in that general vicinity. An average of 400 farmers and farm workers attended, according to his son's account.

Well before that date, in 1915, a Chinese school had been established by Courtland's Chinese. By 1920 if not earlier, Chinatown also boasted a branch of the Bing Kung Tong and of the Chinese Nationalist Party (the Kuomintang or KMT). The school continued in existence until 1940. The KMT endured until slightly after the end of World War II. The Bing Kung Tong branch lasted even longer, although today it is moribund. Most of what remains of Courtland's Chinatown now belongs to Lincoln Chan, son of Chong Chan and another of the handful of Chinese American farmers in the Delta to achieve real success.

Back in the earlier days, Mrs. "David Jones" (pseu.) (whose husband used to

haul potatoes for Chinese potato farmers) recalls that when she was young her family lived near Courtland's Chinatown. An old Chinese lady from Walnut Grove used to take her granddaughter to school in Courtland. One day, Mrs. "Jones" dog bit this granddaughter. The lady approached Mrs. "Jones" family to get a bundle of the dog's hair. Mrs. "Jones" and her family learned later that the lady took the dog's hair home and mixed it with Chinese medicine, ground it into paste, and wrapped it on the girl's wounded leg. Supposedly as a result of this, the little girl recovered from the bite. That girl is still alive and lives in San Francisco, although she is now in her 70's. Mrs. "Jones" also remembers a Chinese girl who was her classmate. This girl learned how to fly an airplane when she was still in her teens. Mrs. "Jones" remembers being very impressed by her courage.

It will have been noted that apart from the above stories, I have made little mention of Chinese wives and daughters in the Delta. Earlier, I pointed out that immigration restrictions made it very difficult for Chinese to bring their wives into the United States. Miscegenation laws, as well as Chinese custom, prevented them from marrying non-Chinese. Merchants were not subject to the same immigration restrictions and many did bring their wives over. But for the average farm laborer and tenant farmers, this was impossible. (Incidently, this contributed greatly to the flourishing of brothels in the Chinatowns.)

For the average Chinese farm laborer, the only realistic way of marrying and starting a family was to make at least one trip back to China, where he would secure and establish a bride. However, this was not a simple process. Marriage for a farm laborer was usually postponed until he could make some money in the United States. For example, one of Locke's retired farm laborers explains he left China at the age of twenty-one. By the time he returned to China to get married he was thirty-five years old. Another farm laborer went back to China to visit his mother in 1920, but it was not until 1927, the second time he went, that he had enough money to get married. In other words, it took him fifteen years to establish himself financially. Some laborers never could afford to go back to get a wife. One of the reasons was insufficient funds, often due to excessive gambling. Gambling certainly was a temptation. One single farm laborer explains that he had no other form of entertainment, and he did not have any relatives around to control him. "If a friend said, 'let's go to gamble', I went with him. It was exciting. When I lost, I went to work again. I could not save my money."

It was always a joyous occasion when a man returned to China to visit his family and relatives after many years of hard work in the United States. If he said that he wanted to marry while he was in China, his family would make all the arrangements including finding a wife, preparing everything for the wedding, negotiating for the dowry, making the banquet reservations, and so forth. When the son finally arrived home, all the activities would take place, but he had to pay for all the expenses. Such a trip could easily exhaust all of one's hard earned money. The farm laborer Wong

Yow confirmed that he had spent about $3,000 for his trip home and marriage in 1935. He paid for his trip tickets, the dowry for the bride's family, and the wedding banquet for his and his bride's families, relatives, and the entire village. He purchased a house and seven acres of rice fields to guarantee that his new wife would be taken care of for her life. As a result, not too long after the wedding ceremony, the husband had to return to the United States because he had to earn more money. In addition, the United States government would only permit him to remain in China for ten or twelve months. Children usually were born after their father returned to the United States. If a couple did not have children, they would usually adopt a son. In either case, the father did not really know his children, who were raised by the mother.

The farm laborer Choi Sun explained that, "I went back to get married, and my eldest daughter was born in 1922 after I came back to America." Choi Sun's eldest daughter, Mrs. Chan continued,

"I remember that I saw my father several times when I was young. I knew that he was my father, but I did not know him in all other aspects. I did not know what he did in America. I knew he was very nice to his family because he supported us and sent money home."

Wong Yow's son explained,

"In all my years before I immigrated to the United States, I remember seeing my father just once. I knew I had a father because my mother talked about him and we received letters and money from him from time to time. When we finally lived together, we could not communicate with each other."

Although many of these laborers had a family back in the old country and remained loyal to their family, they did not actually have any family life here. They were laborers for their family — making money to support those who lived in another world.

As for laborers who had come to the United States illegally, they could not leave this country. Going home to get married was out of the question even if they had saved enough money. In a number of cases, these laborers finally got married after their immigration status was readjusted in the 1950s, although they were in their fifties and sixties by then. They went back to Hong Kong to find a young wife. They were able to obtain wives because on one hand they had money, and on the other there were large numbers of Chinese refugees who escaped from mainland China to Hong Kong in the 1950s. Living conditions in Hong Kong were very difficult, so there were girls willing to marry older men. These marriages were arranged by the girl's relatives in order to get the girl an opportunity to come to the United States in the future.

Chapter 4
Locke, California

Locke is not the first Chinese town established in California. It is not even the only Chinese town that the Delta has known. However, it is the only one to endure until the present day and as such, it is a symbol of an important aspect of the Chinese experience in and contribution to this country. Although the character of the town has changed in aspect several times since its founding, it has always been tied to Delta agriculture.

The town of Locke grew out of a boarding house, a gambling parlor and a saloon established at that location in 1912 by three Chinese entrepreneurs. The rationale behind these three businesses, located about a mile upriver from Walnut Grove, had to do with the packing shed that the Southern Pacific Railroad constructed there in the same year, and the railroad spur which led to it. There was also a dock next to the packing shed. The whole was called Lockeport since it and the surrounding land were owned by the Locke family. The three Chinese businessmen, Chungshan men all, realized that most if not all of the laborers in the packing shed would be Chinese. By locating close to the packing shed, they felt that their businesses were certain to attract adequate customers from among the laborers and indeed that is precisely what happened.

Three businesses located a little beyond the town limits of Walnut Grove, however, do not of themselves constitute a new town. But in 1915, an accidental fire led to the complete destruction of Walnut Grove's Chinatown. The Chinatown had contained large contingents of Sze Yap and Chungshan people, but after the fire many of the Chungshan people decided to build houses and settle next to the three Chungshan businesses at Lockeport. (The rest of the residents of Walnut Grove's Chinatown rebuilt in the former location.) Chief among those who moved to Lockeport was Bing Lee, a merchant. The acknowledged leader of the new settlers, Bing Lee financed the construction of some nine residential houses and opened his own general merchandise store in the new town. The town's name of "Lockeport" was soon shortened to "Locke," or "Lockee" (the latter being the Chinese pronounciation of "Locke").

The residents of the nine houses financed by Bing Lee were families rather than single men, and most were merchants as well. They had had businesses in Walnut Grove's Chinatown prior to the 1915 fire. For the first five or so years after 1915, Locke grew slowly as a few more Chungshan families decided to build there. In addition,

the original boarding house provided living quarters for Chungshan laborers, mostly men who worked in the packing shed. In all cases, the land on which Chinese residences and businesses stood was owned by whites since state law forbade the Chinese immigrants from purchasing land. The Locke family leased the land for the town to the Chinese through a verbal agreement.

The asparagus boom was then in full flower, and by 1920, more and more boarding houses and businesses catering to the Chungshan workers in the asparagus fields were being built. Several entrepreneurs opened canneries in Locke's vicinity during the 1920s, and in 1925 Southern Pacific enlarged the packing shed. Consequently, Locke expanded ever more rapidly. Throughout the 1920s Prohibition also contributed greatly to the economic importance and physical growth of the town. An important "illicit" amusement quarter developed which included gambling parlors, speakeasies, a few opium dens, and several houses of prostitution. The whorehouses were owned, operated, and staffed by whites, but the gambling parlors, speakeasies and opium dens were mostly owned and operated by Chinese. (There were no Chinese prostitutes in Locke because of the respectable Chinese families in the town. However, there were Chinese prostitutes in nearby Walnut Grove.)

Locke was, indeed, quite a lively place in the 1920s. It had a (Chinese-owned) movie theater for several years which showed silent black and white films. A Chinese herbalist dispensed medicine and medical advice. There were six restaurants (two of them served *dim sim* [*yum cha,* a Cantonese kind of snack]), nine grocery stores (two of which operated their own slaughterhouse), a flour mill, a hotel and numerous boarding houses. All of these except the flour mill were owned and operated by Chinese. The mill was run by an East Indian, a Hindu, and catered especially to the growing number of East Indian farm laborers in the Delta. Locke even had its own Christian mission, operated by the Baptists, from 1919 until the 1940s. Ironically, the "wages of sin" that the Baptists hoped to eradicate (money from gambling and the like) provided an important part of the financial support for the mission: gambling house owners were among the most generous contributors to the building of the mission.

The most important of the grocery stores was Yuen Chong, a business which originally operated in Walnut Grove. It had moved to Locke in 1915 and it remains there to this day. The business is a partnership rather than having a single owner. Shares (even half shares) are bought and sold. These shares automatically raised the status of a possessor from that of a laborer to that of a merchant, a crucial difference in terms of immigration status during the days of Chinese Exclusion. Yuen Chong was a major supplier of food and an important source of credit to the Chinese farm laborer work camps and Chinese tenant partnerships which operated in the vicinity of Locke and Walnut Grove. Since the late 1940s, when the Chinese presence in the Delta began its permanent decline, the store has lost its former importance but it has managed to survive whereas the others went out of business, one by one. Another early

business that has survived until the present is the bar/restaurant called "Al the Wops," founded by an Italian and currently much favored by Delta farmers and tourists.

Locke's boarding houses catered primarily to agricultural laborers. The majority of these were Chungshan Chinese, but during the 1920s other groups also became important such as Filipinos, Japanese, and for a time, East Indians. Agricultural laborers fell into two major classifications: permanent, year-round workers and seasonal laborers. The latter were usually people hired to bring in the harvest. During the season, they would live in work camps in the fields but when they were between jobs and during the winter, many lived in boarding houses in Locke or other Delta towns. (Others lived in the cities during the off-season.) Permanent workers, on the other hand, would either live in the boarding houses year round, or had quarters provided for them on the ranches where they worked. Whether permanent or seasonal, many of the farm laborers who lived in the boarding houses supplemented their wages by working part-time in local packing sheds or in nearby canneries (although much cannery work was also done by women).

In addition to the various legitimate businesses, Locke in the 1920s contained the several kinds of illegal enterprises already mentioned. Whorehouses catered to whites as well as non-whites. Gambling joints, owned and operated by Chinese, seem to have been only three in number. They also catered to whites as well as non-whites. In addition to regular Chinese gambling games, one or all of the gambling houses operated a Chinese lottery which had two drawings a day. Lottery tickets from the gambling houses were sold for a commission by most of the restaurants, and by some of the other business establishments. Since the lottery tickets could be purchased almost anywhere, many non-Chinese got the impression that Locke had "countless" gambling halls.

I should mention in passing that Chinese, even those who frown on gambling, generally feel that lotteries are harmless and are not immoral. Certainly many Chinese in California viewed Sacramento's laws against Chinese lotteries as a form of outside interference closely linked to the anti-Chinese movement. The lottery, often called *pai-ho p'iao* or *pak kop piu* utilizes the eighty words (Chinese characters) from a venerable Chinese literary work known as the One Thousand Character classic. The lottery player selects a minimum of ten of the eighty characters. (In the 1920s the average bet was $1.00 to $1.50 for the ten). The lottery house selected (in a complicated but random fashion) twenty characters per drawing. To win, you must have marked at least five of the twenty characters selected. Average winnings ranged from double the bet for five characters to more than 2,000 times the bet if you had correctly marked all twenty. Chinese custom suggested that winners of anything more than the smallest amounts should celebrate by inviting family and friends to a fancy dinner at a restaurant.

During the 1920s, various Chinese social organizations established branches in Locke. The town, itself, hired a night watchman and instituted other cooperative services such as a means of negotiating with the landowners and of handling water rights. The town's communal gardens, where currently the permanent Chinese residents grow vegetables, dates from the late 1920s and early 1930s. Each year as they harvest their crop — Chinese cabbage, snow peas, a leafy vegetable for soup, winter melon, tomatoes, and so forth — some is used fresh, some is dried, and some given to friends or relatives.

The principal social organizations to establish a branch in Locke were the Jan Ying Association and the Kuomintang (also called KMT: the Chinese Nationalist Party.) There was a Chinese school as well, and Walnut Grove's Bing Kung Tong also served the Locke community. The Bing Kung Tong has branches all over the United States. It is a fraternal secret society founded around the turn of the century which has been much involved in gambling. Similar to the other tongs, however, regulating gambling parlors has never been its only concern, as I noted earlier. For example, it helped fill the vacuum created by the absence of family life for the average Chinese immigrant and channeled some of the nationalist feeling that these immigrants entertained with respect to their homeland. It also helped mediate quarrels between members (and most of Locke's inhabitants, both permanent residents and seasonal farm laborers, were members). The Jan Ying Association in many ways duplicated the functions of the Bing Kung Tong. Like the latter, it provided members with a sense of home and family. Its headquarters (like the Bing Kung Tong building) was a place of relaxation and a place where members might learn of a job. Both organizations hosted several annual banquets for members.

There were, however, several important differences between the two organizations. For one thing, membership in the Bing Kung Tong was open to any Chinese man. Only Chungshan men could join the Jan Ying Association. The Bing Kung Tong has had far more members and branches nationwide than the Jan Ying Association which is confined to California. Although the Jan Ying Association has been involved in mediating disputes and helped regulate community life, as long as the Locke community had available branches of both organizations, the Jan Ying Association was less influential and its decisions were less binding than those of the Bing Kung Tong. Locke's Jan Ying Association has been especially important in regulating affairs between Chungshan labor contractors and Chungshan farm laborers. The Bing Kung Tong was more important in general commercial affairs and (in the period before 1950) in the gambling business. Finally, unlike the Bing Kung Tong, the Jan Ying Association has not had really strong ties to national Chinese politics.

The most politically oriented of Locke's associations was the KMT. Locke's branch of this party flourished from the 1920s until the early 1950s. The town KMT headquarters was originally financed by Bing Lee, the merchant who led the move from

Walnut Grove to Locke in 1915. The KMT owed some of its initial strength among Chinese in the Delta to Dr. Sun Yat-sen's visits to the area. Dr. Sun, the revolutionary leader who in 1912 became first provisional president of the newly-established Republic of China, made a couple of trips through the Delta prior to 1912 in order to solicit the support of the Chinese there. Since Dr. Sun came from Chungshan County, Chungshan Chinese responded to his call with special enthusiasm.

As many people know, the progress of the Republic of China was not always smooth. The same statement applies to the KMT, which led the Republic. First the party of Sun Yat-sen and then (after Sun's death in 1925) of Generalissimo Chiang Kai-shek, the KMT in the United States sought to develop a nationalistic spirit among the Chinese here and to secure their aid. Chinese in America have frequently been called upon to donate money to the party and at certain periods were also asked to help develop China's Air Force. Chancy Chew, who was a very successful merchant and Chungshan tenant farmer near Locke, assisted in the purchase of several airplanes in the mid-1920s at the request of the KMT. These were to be used to train pilots and, after the training program ended, were to be sent along with the pilots to China. The training program was launched but never completed because a foe of the KMT set fire to the airplanes several months after their purchase. All of the aircraft, as well as the shed in which they were stored, were totally destroyed.

Other projects of the KMT in Locke and Locke's vicinity met with greater success. As part of its effort to revive and modernize thinking in China, the KMT launched the "New Life Movement" in China in the 1930s. In America, this was reflected by a renewed emphasis on Chinese schools for native born Chinese Americans. The Chinese schools, which provided instruction in the afternoons and evenings, were designed to teach Chinese American children of their Chinese cultural heritage; help them learn to speak, read and write Chinese; and prepare them to pursue a career in China if they found opportunities in America too restricted. Locke had its Chinese school, closely tied to the KMT. Bing Lee was an early organizer and supporter of this school. A later supporter was Joe Shoong, the millionare owner of National Dollar Stores. The school continued in existence, with a few breaks, from the 1920s until the late 1970s. By the 1930s and early 1940s, it was at its height in terms of numbers of students and breadth of instruction.

Another major effort in which Locke's KMT was involved was support for China in her war against Japan (1931-1945). This support was primarily in the form of financial contributions. In addition, one of the generals involved in the Chinese defense of Shanghai traveled through the Delta in 1937. He was honored in all of the Delta's Chinatowns, and his presence generally strengthened community organization in Locke as well as elsewhere.

The town of Locke, and its community organizations, were at their height in the 1920s. In 1930, the Depression hit the town and coincidentally, the pear crop (a mainstay of the local orchards) failed due to the especially cold spring. Asparagus had been in a slow decline since 1925 because of the spread of a disease which affected the plants. The Depression forced the closing of several Delta canneries; the death in 1932 of the only cannery owner who was ethnically Chinese (Thomas Foon Chew) closed yet another. The result was to deprive many of Locke's permanent residents of their means of livelihood and to make life increasingly precarious for the seasonal laborers. That the town did not empty out completely is due to the fact that as bad as was the situation in the Delta, problems elsewhere were even more acute. Many Chinese who had never before engaged in agricultural labor came to Locke and other Delta communities looking for work. Jobs were not always forthcoming, wages were depressed, and the standard of living declined but the town struggled on.

In the 1940s, things improved somewhat. Wages began to rise and, since the economy in general was getting better, fewer unemployed had to seek work in the Delta. This meant that more jobs were available for those who continued to depend on agricultural work. The outbreak of World War II accelerated the trend: not only were some farm workers drafted, but the internment of people of Japanese ancestry had the unintended effect of opening up more jobs (and tenant farms) to Chinese.

However, at the same time a gradual decline in the Delta's Chinese population had begun. The population decline became more rapid in the 1950s as more and more young Chinese Americans became old enough to look for jobs. Far better educated than their parents, they rarely stayed in agricultural districts. By the 1960s, the parents of these young Chinese Americans, and other older immigrants, began to retire as age forced them to slow down. Even though Chinese Exclusion ended in 1943, no new Chinese immigrants have come to the Delta to replace the older agricultural workers. Many of these latter have moved to the cities to be near their children. Some have died. Some have remained in the Delta, living on small pensions or on social security. Locke has gone into a real decline. By the late 1970s, only about one hundred people lived in the town and at the present, the number is closer to fifty.

I have mentioned that non-Chinese have lived in Locke since the 1920s. Today, non-Chinese number about twenty-five people, mostly white. The town's Chungshan Chinese number about forty. The town watchman is long gone. The KMT closed its doors years ago. Of the business establishments, Yuen Chong grocery remains along with several white-owned businesses which cater to tourists. The town would be sliding toward complete obscurity and a rapid demise were it not for a recent controversy which has put it in the center of a fight between a new property owner/developer and several California state and county agencies.

The controversy came about because the new property owners (a husband and

wife from Hong Kong) want to make drastic changes in the area in the name of turning Locke, and that portion of the Delta, into a profit-making monument to Chinese in America. Before their aim could be accomplished, first Sacramento County and then the State of California stepped in to say that the developers' means and methods were wrong. Government planners suggested that perhaps the state should take control of the town in the interest of the public as well as of Locke's residents. The public interest is related to projecting an accurate picture of the Chinese contribution to the Delta. From the state's point of view, the dilemma is how to preserve and display what Locke represents without destroying Locke. Locke's inhabitants, in the meantime, would for the most part like to be left in peace.

It seems unfair to end an account of Locke with a note saying no one quite knows what will happen to it, but that is in fact the case. The alternatives appear radically different: continued slow decline; redevelopment and restructuring to permit preservation as "living history"; radical alterations leading to a new existence as a semi-suburban, semi-commercialized "symbol" of Chinese culture and contributions. So far, no final decision has been reached as to which of these alternatives will prevail. For the time being, Locke is a town of retired Chungshan farm workers and tenant farmers with a leavening of white and other non-Chinese — a town that every weekend is put up for inspection to the tourists who come by car and tour bus to examine it. A small town on the banks of the Sacramento, its aging buildings and the communal gardens out back are surrounded by pear orchards and sloughs. And for better or worse, Locke is the only remaining rural Chinese town in the United States.

Chapter 5

Daily Life of the Delta's Chinese
Farm Laborers and Tenant Farmers

As early as the mid-1860s, agriculture had become the principal occupation and most important means of livelihood in the Sacramento Delta. At first, grain was the main crop. By the 1870s, however, it had become apparent that fruit orchards and truck farms were more profitable. In this century, in the 1920s and 1930s, the most important crops were pears, asparagus, onions and potatoes. All but asparagus remain important to this day, especially pears.

From the very beginning, most Delta farms have been very large, far too large for the owner to operate by himself. Instead, the owner hired farm laborers, or leased the land out to farm tenants, or sometimes both. During the harvest season, the need for laborers was particularly acute; even tenant farmers had to hire harvest hands in considerable numbers. At the peak of the harvest, several thousand farm laborers were routinely required to bring in the crops. A significant proportion of these farm laborers were Chinese.

Chinese agricultural laborers in the Delta worked both in the orchards and on the truck farms. The number of Chinese farm workers in the Delta has varied through time, since workers of other nationalities (especially Japanese, Filipinos, and Mexicans) have also been available. In this century, the high point for Chinese workers came during the Depression, when as many as 2,000 worked on Delta farms during the harvest season. Well over half of these were agricultural laborers; the rest were tenant farmers. Most Chinese from Chungshan County worked in the orchards (although there were exceptions). And a very large proportion of these lived in Locke.

Except for a relatively small number who were permanent crew members, these farm laborers from Chungshan County were seasonal workers, migrating from one orchard to the next depending on which crop was in season. Whether seasonal workers or permanent crew members, during the summer they were asked to prune, weed, and cut blight, as well as harvest the fruit. In the winter, the permanent crews wove baskets (to be used in the summer for the harvest), repaired ladders, milked cows, and conducted the general maintenance of the orchards. Such activities kept them busy eleven to twelve hours a day. For the most part, they worked in groups headed

by a bilingual Chinese foreman, the man who originally recruited them for the job. He distributed their pay, negotiated their work conditions, and transmitted the owner's instructions. The owner provided the laborers with some form of housing (tents, a bunkhouse, or the like) while the foreman usually located a cook to provide the workers with food.

The Chinese who became tenant farmers had slightly different responsibilities. Most joined tenant partnerships with other Chinese. Leasing land from white farmer/landlords, they grew the usual crop for that given piece of land, i.e., if the land was planted in orchard, they grew and harvested the fruit. If the land was being used as a truck farm, the tenants grew potatoes and onions. Although I mentioned above that most of Locke's residents and most other Chinese from Chungshan County specialized in orchard work, many Delta tenant farmers leased both orchard land and truck farms. They seemed to expect most of their income to come from the orchards, however. After the harvest, the tenants gave a specific portion of their profits to the landlord. Originally, these share rental contracts were verbal agreements, but later written ones were more common. The landlord, in return, provided many of the chemicals and farm implements needed. Sometimes he provided credit as well, although credit was also available from the Chinese community. The landlord was also concerned with the development of the crop, as well as its market price.

Picking and spraying in the orchards was done manually. For this reason, the trees had to be of a size and shape to allow for the most efficient methods of maintenance. Farmers and farm laborers pruned pear trees, for example, to allow "ladder space:" a spot for the ladder so that the worker could reach the greatest area of the tree from one place. The Chungshan farmers limited the height of the trees so that pickers could reach the fruit on the highest branches. Branches were pruned to allow sufficient sunlight so that the pears matured evenly. Excess fruit was cut out to leave the remaining pears enough room to develop more fully. Through these pruning procedures, the pears developed into large, excellent fruit. Before mechanization became widespread, workers sprayed trees with ten-foot long bamboo poles which had brass tubing inside. Pumps and spray tanks spread the insecticide to all parts of the tree. Pruners facilitated this procedure by trimming the tree in such a way that the sprayer could cover the tree well without having branches obstruct his work.

The Delta's Chungshan farmers and agricultural laborers were patient and conscientious. While irrigating the orchards (often called ranches), the men stayed from sunrise to sunset managing the water flow. Irrigation of a field took place section by section, and the workers and tenants used watering methods they had learned in China. The tenant farmers improved their ranches and worked on them all year round. In the 1920s most work was done by fieldhands; any hauling was done by horses. It was not until the late 1930s and the 1940s that trucks began to be used in the fields. Life for tenant farmers, as well as for agricultural laborers, was more difficult in the

34

early days than it is now.

These farm laborers, and the tenant farmers who used to be farm laborers, remember the hard days of the 1920s when their wages were "$1.00 a day." Some couldn't even find a job in the Delta. In the 1910s, things had been slightly better. Then a man could expect $1.50, or even $1.75 for a twelve-hour day of work. However, even then work was not always steady and an annual salary of $300-$500 was quite common.

Wages did not approach $1.50 a day again until the final years of the Depression. But by 1940, the pay rate had begun to rise dramatically. Wong Yow is a retired farm laborer who has lived in Locke for over half a century. During all that period, he kept a detailed diary complete with financial records. From him we learn that between 1938 and 1941, when World War II economics changed the picture, his pay rate almost doubled, going from $1.50 to almost $3 a day. However, over the same period his annual salary only rose by some twenty-five percent, to $738.50 in 1941, evidently because he worked for fewer hours.

After the attack on Pearl Harbor and the United States entry into World War II, his salary improved greatly. Wong Yow's annual wages were never lower than $1,500 from 1942 on, and by the mid-1950s they were as high as $3,500 after room and board had been subtracted out. (Room and board for Locke's farm laborers ran about $1,000 annually at this time.) For the last ten years prior to his retirement in 1967, Wong Yow's income and expenses for room and board remained at approximately this same rate.

In spite of the improvement, these are obviously very modest sums of money. Yet in spite of their situation, many of the farm laborers managed to take care of clothing and recreational expenses, pay their taxes, send money back to their families in China, and even have something left over as savings. However, this meant staying away from the gambling parlors whose attractions proved too strong for many of the farm laborers to resist.

Wong Yow is one of those who did resist, and by living frugally (his wardrobe and furniture have always been severely limited), during the 1950s and 1960s he was able to send an average of fifteen to twenty percent of his salary to his family in Hong Kong, and save an average of fifty percent.

What happened to the money the farm laborers saved? Many used it to buy land and houses back in China where they hoped to retire. (The Communist triumph in 1949, however, resulted in the loss of all these investments.) Some was used to pay for passage back to China and for a dowry and wedding in the home village, in order to secure a wife for the farm laborer. Some of the laborers used their savings to invest in a tenant farming partnership with other Chinese in the Sacramento Delta. Some

used their money to bring their relatives over from China to the United States, and some invested in small businesses or in land purchases in the Delta.

Chinese farm laborers in the Delta, like most of California's agricultural workers, found that the hours were longer and workload heavier in the seven months beginning in April and ending at the end of October. Wong Yow, for example, worked an incredible 3,414 hours in the year 1959 as shown by his diary. This was typical of all of the Delta's Chinese farm laborers. (For comparison, a fifty-hour work week with one week of vacation would come to somewhat under 2,600 hours a year.) Of these 3,414 hours, some 2,348 represent his hours for the April through October period. Not all of the work was done at the same orchard. Wong Yow routinely worked for two orchards at once, and during the summer might work for as many as four, as well as putting in some hours at a local fruit cannery. Up until the past decade, the minimum work day was ten to twelve hours. As a rule, Wong Yow and the other Chinese farm laborers got up at 5:30 in the morning, cleaned up, ate breakfast, and went to the orchards at 6:00 a.m. They had two tea breaks (fifteen minutes each), one at 9:00 a.m. and one at 3:00 p.m. Lunch time was one and one-half hours long, beginning at 11:30 a.m. The laborer's day ended around six or seven in the evening; sometimes, not until eight. In contrast, the retired Chinese laborers in Locke say that farm laborers at the present time work for eight hours (from 5:30 a.m. to 2:00 p.m. with half an hour for lunch).

Today, there are fewer than ten Chinese American families farming in the Sacramento Delta, and none live in Locke. However, Chinese American farmers still compete successfully with others. They reflect the contribution of Chinese in the last hundred years to Delta farming. Lincoln Chan, who has orchards in Courtland, California, is known as the pear king of California. He grows 100 acres of Bartlett pears. In addition, he produces tomatoes, sugar beets, corn, wheat and safflower on a total of 2,500 acres, leased from fifteen separate landowners. He also owns many acres himself. Mr. Chan says that in the 1950s he was farming 5,000 acres. He is very pleased that all three of his children are interested in agriculture.

In general, Locke's residents remember that Chinese in the Sacramento Delta were not as badly treated as they were elsewhere in California. They were not subject to violent attacks, for example, as they were even in such relatively nearby areas as Sacramento and Stockton. However, a few elders still remember the county tax collectors who suddenly appeared in the restaurant or on the ranch to catch Chinese for the "head tax" (poll tax). Ow Hoi-Syu recalls that sometimes when Chinese recognized and saw the county officer at the ranch during the laborers' mealtime, they would hide immediately. The table would have bowls of unfinished rice and other dishes. The laborers were very afraid of government officers checking into their status. Even though the "head tax" and anti-Chinese sentiment had generally come to an end by World War II, when I interviewed them some worried that the information they gave

me might somehow cause them problems with the government (especially immigration) officials.

By and large, however, American farmers and landowners in the Delta have been concerned with their land and crops. They realized that Chinese labor was needed on their ranches and farms. Therefore, they have traditionally been reasonably sympathetic to the Chinese. The contact between Chinese and Americans was most direct in the case of tenant farmers who lived on the American ranches, and Chinese merchants, labor contractors, and foremen, who acted as intermediaries between Americans and the Chinese workers. American farmers usually did not have direct contact with the Chinese laborers, since the latter did not speak English well and went from job to job, from ranch to ranch. Their work was supervised by Chinese foremen or labor contractors.

Chinese tenant farmers and their families lived on the ranches, however, so the opportunity for concern and communication was greater. Tenant farmer's children and the American farmer's children sometimes played together. Some ranch owners got to like their tenants so well that they helped provide the tenants' children with educational opportunities. Many offered the tenants "permanent" tenant's rights.

Jack Chew recalls that in the Delta area there were few actual fights between Chinese boys and white boys. However, this was partly because Chinese and white children had separate schools. The only time Chinese and white students came into contact with each other was when they played ball at an inter-school sports activity.

Some whites worked for Chinese. "David Jones" (pseu.) recalls that he hauled potatoes for five cents a sack. He was hired by Chinese to haul potatoes because he could haul it much faster than Chinese could. He had a truck and drove it to the field, loaded potatoes on the truck and then brought it to the pier to ship to San Francisco. (Chinese haulers at that time still used horses and wagons to do the transporting.) "David Jones" said he had no problem working with Chinese.

On the other side of the coin, "Paul Brown" (pseu.) recalls that his family has had Chinese people on their ranch for many years; six to eight were permanent, year-round workers. His father leased land to a Chinese man who was a former schoolmate of his. This former schoolmate ran a store in Courtland, and leased the farm land to grow onions. "Paul Brown" remembers that the Chinese orchard workers had a camp in back of the orchard. During the summer they slept on boards in the basement of the house in order to keep cool. In their bunkhouse was a kerosene stove to keep them warm in the winter. For cooking they had a homemade brick fireplace with a big pot in the middle, fired by wood. The ceiling above it was black with soot. Occasionally he would go to the bunkhouse to eat. As a boy he would ride along on the wagon as the Chinese workers loaded the baskets full of pears to be trans-

Table 1

Hours Spent Per Year on Specific Tasks Based on Wong's Diary, 1959

Job Number (by order of importance)	Job Description	Hours/Year
1*	Weeding	925
2	Irrigation	589
3	Pruning	577
4	Transporting fruit	337
5*	Cutting blighted branches	190
6	Transporting blighted branches	106
7	Transporting poultry feed	101
8	Repairing crates	88
9	Transporting crates	77
10	Night watch	64
11	Transporting branches	59
12	Planting trees	40
13*	Supporting tree branches	40
14*	Adding diesel oil to burners	40
15*	Aeration of soil	37
16*	Removing other branches affecting growth of fruit trees	24
17	Repairing ladders	24
18	Transporting lumber	21
19	Fertilizing	21
20	Gardening	18
21	Dumping garbage	14
22	Transporting ladder	9
23	Repairing toilet	5
24	Cutting trees	4
25	Harvesting corn for chicken feed	2
26	Miscellaneous	3
	Total hours	3,414

*Wong's explanation of jobs.

Table 2

Monthly Working Hours and Work Locations Based on Wong's Diary, 1959

Place	Month												Total Hours
	Jan	Feb	Mar	Apr	May	Jun	Jul	Aug	Sep	Oct	Nov	Dec	
Orchard 1	*101	61	160	262	134	218	248	204	157	287	192	124	2,168
2	107	78	50	33	88	47	46	75	161	37	40	50	812
3					88				5				93
4				5		24	28	30	41	31	24	89	272
5						5							5
Cannery						23	31	10					64
Total	208	159	210	295	315	317	353	319	359	360	256	263	3,414

*Number indicates hours

This table is self-explanatory. Orchard 1 was Mr. Wong's main location of work. The Peak harvest time--April through October--show that he worked very hard, not only at five orchards, but also in a cannery.

ported to the river dock. Most of the men spoke Chinese among themselves and very little English, except for the crew leader, whose job it was the deal with the owner.

"Paul Brown" had a tenant, Sum Yen Jang, whom he considers to be a good friend. Sum Yen Jang still works a little on the ranch, but he can't do too much anymore because of his arthritis. He worked on "Paul Brown's" ranch for fifty years.

In addition, "Paul Brown" occasionally sees some of the other Chinese who used to work on his farm, because he is invited to the annual spring banquet in Locke. There he chats with his old friends and finds out what has been happening to them since he last saw them.

George R. Adams recalls that his grandfather leased land to Chinese. The tenants came from the Chinese section of the Delta towns. All lived on the ranch during their employment. The ranch provided bunkhouses for them; the bunkhouses had their own kitchens. The landowner told the Chinese how to do the work that needed to be done. If a farming project was a large one, three or four Chinese tenant farmers would go into the venture as partners.

In his own time, George Adams recalls that a lot of opium was smoked on the ranch when he was young. He also remembers that his family had two brothers as a set of tenants at one time. These brothers stayed until about 1945. Both were bachelors. One brother was constantly being chased by the *tongs*. (The other was not involved.) Sometimes this brother would have to hide out with George Adams' family in order to escape the "hatchet men" who would come onto the Adams' ranch. The *tong* men even ran the Adams off the land at times in order to get at the Chinese they were looking for. (The Adams never called the sheriff about the *tong* men; they just let them cool off and go on their way.) This was all prior to 1925; after that time the *tongs* gradually changed and became less violent.

When George Adams was growing up (around 1907-1911), all of his playmates were Chinese. This was around Courtland, about ten miles from Locke. In school only the first three or four grades in elementary school were segregated. After these grades, all went to the same school. George remembers that the Chinese were good students. Most of his former Chinese (actually Chinese American) classmates went on to become professionals. Their parents stayed on the ranches to work until they retired. George Adams recalls that when he was a child, some people in the area teased Orientals although he never did. In the main, he feels that interpersonal relations between Chinese and whites were good. As an adult, George found that most landowners were opposed to Chinese Exclusion (which ended in 1943). They liked the Chinese and needed them as workers in their orchards.

Life for the Chinese farm laborers and tenant farmers was certainly not too easy, but it was not too harsh either. Locke's residents had to work hard, but they could get by and except during the Depression, they could even save money if they didn't gamble too much. Their style of living was reasonably healthy. Although most lacked families in the Delta, their fellow workers were usually congenial, and whites in the area maintained reasonably friendly relations. Finally, it was possible to advance from a farm laborer to a tenant farmer or even small businessman or landowner.

Part II: In Their Own Words

It is fitting, in this second half of the book, to present a few of the interviews I gathered from people who were particularly informative, especially prominent, or most typical. The most difficult part of this process has been to decide who to include and who not to include, since each person I interviewed provided valuable insights of one kind or another. I would like here to beg the forebearance of those not included and assure them that the information they provided has been incorporated into the first part of this book. Furthermore, many will find their names listed in the Acknowledgements.

Most of the people I have included here are in their sixties. More than half were born in China, while the others come from California and grew up in Locke, or lived there for many years. More than half live in Locke at the present time, including two of the people in chapter six and all those in chapter eight. Most of those I have included are men, but there are also two women. And finally, all of these people have in one way or another been connected with Delta farming. For most, the connection has been direct but in two cases, I have chosen people involved in an industry that depended for its profits upon the spendable income of farm laborers and tenant farmers.

Chapter 6

A Farm Laborer, a Tenant Farmer
and a Wealthy Farmer

(Wong Yow, So Yung Ng, and Lum Bunn Fong)

Wong Yow*

My name for many years has been Yow Wong, although I was born Buck-Sing Wong. I was born in China in 1900 in the village of Yuen Fung about three Chinese miles from Shek Kei, the county seat of Chungshan. I have lived in Locke for many years. My mother died when I was hine years old (by Chinese reckoning), so my aunts raised me because my father had emigrated to North America. I spent the first twenty-one years of my life in China. I went to school for several years (I remember the tuition was $3 [Chinese] a year). I also worked at odd jobs which didn't require much skill, such as vegetable gardening. When I was eighteen I began to learn woodworking, but found that I didn't like the craft.

My father followed in the footsteps of his great grandfather and grandfather who both came to the United States. My father was about forty years old when he emigrated. He first went to Mexico, but while he was working there some friends told him that work was more plentiful in the United States, and wages were higher. So he found a company in San Francisco that would sponsor his entrance into the country. The company was named Kim Kee, which was similar to Kim Yick and Kim Sang — stores that were allowed to recruit Chinese workers from abroad.

My father often talked of wanting to bring his son to the United States. He searched until he found a merchant named Mr. Wong who would sponsor me. My father paid that man $1,650. The merchant, my "paper father," arranged for me to come with another man who was my "paper brother." I was given a document listing me as the merchant's son, and declaring that I was entering the United States as a student. In 1921 I arrived at Angel Island from Hong Kong on the ship *Nile*. I had a small suitcase with some clothes.

---

*This interview will also be published, in a different form, in *California History* during 1984.

Two events stand out in my memory of life on Angel Island. There was a Chinese interpreter called "Gwongtauh Lou" (baldheaded man) whom all the interviewees feared. Everyone agreed he was mean. I also remember I heard that there were two "brothers" in camp. The officials knew that they had had a banquet at home before they came to the United States, and that a chicken had been slaughtered for the feast. An officer asked each brother separately the color of the chicken's feathers. The younger brother answered yellow, the older black. Based on their conflicting testimonies, the authorities proved that the two were not brothers and deported them.

At that time the immigration regulations had been changed, and the conditions were better than previously. While I was on Angel Island, I attended class to learn a little English. At mealtime everyone ate in a common dining hall. I did not see any fighting and quarreling among the Chinese. At my interview, the interpreter was a nice person. The officers asked me which room I lived in at home, which room my "brother" lived in, how the furniture in the house was arranged, etc. They didn't ask too many questions, interrogating me about half an hour. My answers were all correct and matched my "brother's," so they approved my papers. After the interview I had to stay a few more days to be examined by American physicians. The doctors examined me and looked for hookworm disease, but they did not take X-rays.

When I got off Angel Island, I went to San Francisco where some people from my village met me and took me to Locke. My father did not come to pick me up because there were *tong* wars then in San Francisco's Chinatown. So I went to Locke on the night ship, which we Chinese called "Gwoji teng" (a ship for transporting fruit).

When I first came to the Delta, I lived with my real (as opposed to "paper") father in Walnut Grove. At that time there were many boarding houses around town. For daily rates they charged 50ᶜ a meal, which included water and a place to sleep for the night. Lodgers did not have to pay immediately but were allowed to postpone payment until they received their paychecks from their jobs. My father and I lived in a small room in one of those boarding houses. For $5 a month we got two beds and a place to cook. When we were working we took our meals at the ranch, but when we didn't work we gathered dry wood and cooked for ourselves. We lived in that room for three years, until my father returned to China in 1924.

During our three years together, my father worked for the King family in Courtland. The first few years in the Delta I did not have a steady job but took what work I could find. Besides working in Walnut Grove and Courtland, I sometimes went to Lodi to harvest grapes. There I was recruited for the job of harvesting hops. The contractor, Gwong Sang Cheung, transported the workers to camp by car. There were forty to fifty of us. While we were there we lived in camps set up on a grassy meadow. Our employers provided the food and hired a cook to feed us. The maximum amount of hops I could harvest in a day was 600 pounds.

44

I harvested hops for two years, then I worked for another man for about ten years, traveling between Sutter Island and Lodi to my different jobs. On Sutter Island I picked fruit, pruned trees, and irrigated. During August and September I went to Lodi to harvest grapes, returning to Sutter Island in October.

In the evening after work I did not have much to do. After washing clothes and taking a shower I usually went straight to bed. Sometimes I read newspapers. Like me, other workers did not have much recreation. When it rained, I did not have to work, but I did not get paid for that day. We felt that working was contentment enough. Occasionally on Sundays our employer would take us to Locke or Walnut Grove by car, so that we could shop or find entertainment. Some gambled. I would shop or have my hair cut, and once in awhile I went to the movies. We were so happy and excited at the opportunity of going to town. Sometimes we would sit on benches on the sidewalk, just watching people and talking. Because we were all men on the ranch, we saw only two women regularly, the boss' wife and daughter. When we went to town, we saw more. We usually stayed until nightfall, then the contractor would come to take us back to the ranch.

During the Great Depression my wages were about ten cents an hour, but I didn't care how little they were as long as I had a job. If I made $1 a day, I could still save some of it because the cost of living was so low at the time. Furthermore, I seldom spent money on myself. I worked all day, ate, read the Chinese newspaper and slept. I didn't smoke or gamble; my only expense was my barber. I was interested in earning money to send home to China and to save. Until 1927 I was still repaying my father the money he had spent for my immigration. After he retired to China in 1924, I sent him money to support my stepmother and my younger brothers. I got married when I returned to China in 1935, so when I returned to the Delta in 1936 I had to work to support my wife as well as my father's family in China.

Money that I didn't send home I deposited in banks such as Alex Brown in Walnut Grove, the American Trust Company in San Francisco, and the Bank of America in Stockton. It took me fourteen years (1921-1935) to save enough money to return to China. From my savings I was also able to buy a house for my father's family to live in. When I went home I bought seven acres of rice fields at 400 Chinese *yuan* an acre [about $115 US dollars]. I used my savings again when I made my second trip back in 1947, buying back the first house I had purchased from my father, buying another house for my stepmother and acquiring more farm land. This time I bought an acre of lichee orchard for 900 *yuan* [about $259 US dollars] and another ten acres of rice fields in the village of Cheung Kai for 1,000 *yuan* an acre [about $288 US dollars].

After I returned from China in 1947, I again worked in Courtland. In 1951 I worked in Locke, and from 1952 until my retirement in 1968 I worked for Dennis Leary, occasionally taking off time to work other places. I lived on his ranch and

45

walked to Walnut Grove to work since he did not provide transportation. The walk took about half an hour.

Once I remember the workers wanted a raise. The boss, however, did not want to give us one so he pulled a trick on us. He raised our wages by fifty cents a day and at the same time increased our food expenses by fifty cents. We though we would get better food to justify the increased prices. (A food company took over the food service for him at his ranch.) Yet on Sundays when we did not work we also did not get paid but still had to pay the additional fifty cents for the food, so we were actually losing money. Despite this, our employer treated us well. He was humorous even though we did not quite understand his language.

When my father retired to China he remarried. His new wife was about my age, and my brothers did not get along well with her. My father wanted to leave the first house I had bought to his second wife but my brothers objected, wanting him to sell it instead. I realized there was too much disharmony within the family so I bought the house back from my father, giving him cash so that he could divide it into seven shares. After my brothers got their shares, however, they still stayed in the house. Because my stepmother did not want to stay with the rest of the family, I bought her another house when I was in China in 1947.

On my first visit back to China in 1935 I got married. My wife was only sixteen years old at the time. My relatives made all the arrangements. We took a wedding picture which included all my relatives (my father, stepmother, my brothers, sister-in-law, and half-brothers) at one of the studios in the village of Shek Kei. The picture now hangs on my living room wall. We also had a big banquet for all our relatives, friends and neighbors. It was a big event in my life, and it was really exciting to see so many people attend.

After a short stay with my new bride, I had to leave her in China and return to the Delta to earn a living to support her, my family and myself. With these added responsibilities I really needed to work again. Moreover, I had spent almost all the money I had saved during the past fourteen years.

In 1949 my wife left China for Hong Kong after the Communist takeover. At that time I did not have enough money to bring her to the United States to join me. Due to the [Chinese Communist] revolution I lost all my investments in China. Although I was approaching my fifties, a time when most Chinese would begin retiring, the unexpected changes in China made me afraid to go back to retire there. Moreover, my investment losses in China forced me to continue working as a laborer in the Delta area to support my family, so I had to give up my hope of retiring at that age. Since I was away from my wife for many years, it was difficult for us to have children. I always sent money home and made sure they had enough food and clothing.

In 1957 when I had again saved enough money, I returned to Hong Kong. At that time I adopted my son and I bought a house for them to live in. It was not a single dwelling but a unit of an apartment building. The apartment unit was located in a nice area for a mid-income family and it cost $7,000 U.S. There were three bedrooms and a living room. My wife and children occupied one bedroom and the living room. The other two rooms were rented out to help subsidize our children's living and school expenses.

In 1967 the Red Guard movement in Hong Kong created a chaotic situation. The Hong Kong government hesitated to take immediate action to counter riots throughout the city. Economic conditions deteriorated and housing prices plummeted. At the time a house was not easy to sell, but because of the unstable political situation I urged my wife to come to the United States. I hired a lawyer to handle all immigration matters, and we finally sold the apartment unit for H.K. $40,000 — $8,000 H.K. less than we had paid ten years before. Today I wish I had not sold the apartment in Hong Kong. It would now have a value of at least a quarter of a million Hong Kong dollars. [When he mentioned that, he looked at me and smiled, although he did not regret the decision that he had made.]

In 1968 my wife and our children came to the United States. My son was eleven years old then. I was sixty-eight. I retired and moved off the ranch. Then I bought a house in Locke for the whole family, and settled down here.

Since I was retired I had to watch how I spent my savings. My wife and children were not accustomed to this kind of environment — so different from Hong Kong's. My wife had not worked in China or Hong Kong and she and the children did not know about my work. People in Hong Kong admired them because their husband and father was in America sending them money each month for their expenses. How lucky they were! Now they saw my living conditions, the kind of work that I did, the way I earned the money that I sent for them to spend however they wished. I had been frugal all my life; they had been accustomed to buying things. Naturally, I was still concerned about the way I spent my money. This concern created some friction between my family and me. Therefore, my wife went to work in the cannery during the harvest season because she wanted to have extra money to spend. Later, I came to feel that she was not totally happy while she lived in Locke. Some years later she became deaf, and in 1978 was killed by a garbage truck while it was backing up to the back of the house.

So Yung Ng (1897-1984)

I was born in Dung village, Chungshan County, in China and have lived in Locke since 1959. When I was in my teens I worked in my uncle's orchard. He grew many kinds of fruits such as peaches, plums, lichees, loquats, bananas, oranges and

tangerines. It was very difficult to make a living during those days in China. There was not enough food and few jobs and I only got ten cents for a whole day's work as a farm laborer. Nonetheless, I was considered lucky just to have been hired by a relative. Because of the conditions many people decided to leave their home country, China, and go abroad to make a living.

In 1920, when I was twenty-three years old I decided to go abroad. As far as I knew there were three ships taking Chinese passengers from Hong Kong to the American continent. These three ships were the *China,* the *Nile* and the *Nanking.** The *Nanking* was the biggest one among the three and I took it. On board this ship there were about 1,100 Chinese. About 500 of them were going to Cuba and about 500 were going to Mexico, but less than twenty were coming to the United States.

I left Hong Kong to go to Mexico. I paid eighty dollars for the ship's fare. The ship went to San Francisco. It took thirty days and nights to complete the trip. After arriving in San Francisco I was sent to Angel Island to wait for the next train to Mexico. Because I was not entering the United States I didn't have to be interrogated by United States immigration officers.

I stayed on Angel Island for about ten days. There were about 800 Chinese retained in the camp. Many Chinese were from Sze Yap in China. There were men, women and children. I still recall many instances of unfair treatment toward the Chinese who were waiting to enter the United States. I remember one of the guards who was yelling "Yak la!" (eat now!) during meal times, and all the hungry people who could get trampled to death by the hordes as they pushed into the dining hall. They were served rice but the food was very poor and minimal. After supper we were shoved into the barricaded area for a short exercise period. During those ten days I heard many things about Chinese who committed suicide and some who were forced to stay there for three years. I felt the Americans didn't treat us as human beings. Chinese came here to join their families, but they were treated like prisoners and many events irrelevant to immigration were used to make them ineligible to be admitted into the country. I recall there was a Chinese who came from my village and stayed for three years. He could speak some English so he helped some newly arrived people fill out their forms or write their names and addresses. I felt I was lucky that I was not coming to the United States directly.

After the miserable days at Angel Island we finally arrived in Mexicali, Mexico by train from San Francisco. Mexicali was called "Sun Fa Kay" (New Flower Flag) by the Chinese. Our treatment in Mexicali was more humane than in the United States.

---

*These three were the ships of the China Mail Steamship Line, a Chinese-owned steamship line with headquarters in San Francisco.

I stayed there for eighteen months. After my arrival I found there were already Chinese district associations and family clans established to help these newly arrived Chinese. I joined the Chungshan Association. There were no houses — all the Chinese lived in tents. Each district or family association had its own area in which to set up its peoples' tents. I was told to get a tent large enough for two people to live in. If a person didn't have money the store would give credit and get payment later. Some people were even supplied with rice and food until they could get a job. The day after our arrival we were invited to a tea house for lunch. In the tea house all kinds of special Chinese *dim sum* were served. One more thing we were asked to do was to send a message home to let our family know that we had arrived safely. The association had someone to help to do this and a donation of fifty cents was collected from those who could afford it. Chinese groceries were also available in Chinese stores such as Wah Mook, Yee Jee Ying and Yee Dai Ley.

Only cotton was grown in Mexicali. Mexicali had just recently become a cotton-growing region. The district was very hot — on summer mornings it was over 85 degrees and in the afternoon the temperature reached as high as 110 degrees. Even though it was so hot, we Chinese farm laborers didn't have any choice but to work in the fields. It was the only kind of job available for new arrivals. I got a job in a cotton growing company and worked in the field. In this place the Chinese worked ten hours each day from 8 a.m. to 6 p.m. They got $3 for each 100 pounds of cotton picked. The cotton was picked and put into a long sack. These sacks of cotton were piled into a horse-pulled wagon and then transported to a place which processed the cotton fibers. Oil was extracted from cotton seeds for cooking. Then the cotton products were shipped to the United States. This cotton plantation received loans from American banks.

In the beginning the price of cotton was fifty cents a pound so the business could support a lot of people working in this area. After World War I the price of cotton dropped to ten cents per pound due to low demand. Many businesses went bankrupt and some Chinese workers didn't even get paid. Because there were no more jobs many Chinese workers had to find a way to leave this area. Many Chinese attempted to come to the United States.

Around 1921 more than 800 Chinese wanted to be smuggled into the United States from the Mexicali area. Some illegal companies took over this smuggling business. There were American smugglers everywhere, and we Chinese had to pay a high price to the smuggling companies in order to get a chance to enter the country. The price for being smuggled to San Francisco was about $500 per person with no guarantee of safety. Sometimes arguments might arise between two companies because of competition. The chances of being attacked, killed, or getting arrested by the police were present at every stage of the process. The victims were always the innocent Chinese workers who just wanted to get a job to survive. Among the 800 chinese in 1921 some

were killed, some were caught and sent back to China and some came to the United States safely.

In my own case I paid $500 to an American smuggler. Actually it was paid by my cousin who sponsored me, a Mr. Choi Sun, who was already working in Courtland, California. I boarded a ship in Mexico around 6 a.m. and I arrived in San Francisco safely. My cousin came to meet me and paid the fee; then we took a ship and came up to Sacramento because at that time there was no bus to Sacramento. I still remember one of the Chinese sailors who worked on that ship.

After I arrived in Courtland I first worked as a farm laborer. Mr. Kong Geng-Hoon was the labor contractor who handled and recruited me to work. During the summers I picked fruit and during the winters I pruned the fruit trees.

But by 1930, when Herbert Hoover was the president of the United States, the economy had started going downhill and the Chinese residents in the Delta couldn't get full-time employment. Many people only found part-time jobs that lasted three to five weeks, and then had to look for another job again. People were trying to do anything they could to survive. Some resorted to fishing. I remember that perches were usually what they caught.

The situation didn't improve until 1933 when Franklin Roosevelt became president. After that Chinese residents were covered under the Social Security Act and jobs were more plentiful than before. But the Chinese people still had to work very hard. At that time the pay rate was about $1 U.S. per day (including meals) and people had to work for eleven hours a day.

Meanwhile, some Chinese worked as tenant farmers on the large ranches owned by Americans. Usually the American landowners provided all the agricultural equipment and mechanical maintenance while the Chinese provided the labor. The profit was usually split fifty-fifty between the two sides. But there were some cases in which the Chinese workers were unfairly treated. For instance, some landlords would only give twenty-five percent or even twenty percent of the profit to these hard working Chinese.

During the Depression I could not find a job in any orchard. For this reason I worked at Yuen Chong Market for a period of time. Not until the start of World War II when Japanese workers were put into relocation camps were Chinese farm laborers in demand again. Also, the military recruited many former farm laborers. Illegal residents were encouraged by the government to join the army. It was my chance to change my status so I enlisted. I got drafted and was classified 1-A. But my boss at Yuen Chong Market (in Locke) wanted me to continue working for him. He told me that he would increase my wages from $100 per month to $105 per month. I replied, "No." Unless I could get $300 a month I would not continue to work at the market.

50

I felt my opportunity had come. If I didn't take this chance, I would be poor all my life. At the same time I was asked to become a member of a tenant farming partnership and farm for Mr. Paul Emmet. I thought it was a good idea because during the war the price for food would rise. So I left Yuen Chong Market and joined the other two partners to farm.

Mr. Paul Emmet had about 300 acres. He agreed to provide all the equipment and materials needed. In return we provided the labor. I worked together with my partners for a few years until one of the partners, Mr. Lee Jok Nam, died. Since Mr. Lee had worked for several decades he insisted what he did was right and we listened to this old boss. But I discovered that the farm was not operated properly. After Mr. Lee's death, Mr. Emmet wanted me to continue to farm for him. I told Mr. Emmet that I would have to make a lot of changes in the orchard. Mr. Emmet didn't object.

When Mr. Lee was operating the farm he wouldn't release water during April and July. At that time the orchard only yielded about 100 tons of pears. Much of this fruit was the size of a candle because it was not fully developed. After I took over the full responsibility of operating the orchard I applied some of my knowledge and skills to its management. For example, I released water to flood the orchard three to four times during April and July. Moreover, I realized that the climate of China and the United States was very different. In China the weather is hot and wet during the summer. From day to night the temperature does not change that much. On the other hand, in the Delta area it is hot and dry during the summer. The temperature in the day is quite different from the temperature at night. The methods of farming should not be the same in both places. Also, in Courtland, the orchards usually cover a large piece of land but in China the orchards are divided into small sections and built on different levels. Many water ditches must be built in order to get rid of excess water after summer rains. Sometimes water gates are built to control the water flow from one section to another section. Due to the weather and poor knowledge of farming, fruit farming in China didn't produce good yields compared to here. I was pleased I worked here. Can you believe what happened? The first year after I began managing the farm, the crop yields increased from 100 tons to 160 tons. During the following years it even reached 180 tons and the price was $100 per ton. This was my opportunity. My boss and I made some money during those years.

My boss, Mr. Emmet, wanted to run for county supervisor, and so gave a big party on his thirty-fifth wedding anniversary. Many people were invited including another Chinese and me. During the party, my boss took me up in front of his guests and announced that if he didn't have me working for him he wouldn't be having today's party. I felt very great and honored at this occasion. I became popular because of my boss' words and many orchard owners wanted me to work for them.

After that I became well known in the Courtland area. There were one or two Chinese who were jealous of my success and tried to ruin me by having Americans write letters in English stating that I smoked opium. My boss showed me the letters, but I told him I had hay fever and asthma very badly between April and July. I said that if I didn't smoke opium I couldn't farm. Moreover, I had taken allergy shots but they hadn't helped at all. I told him that smoking opium hadn't become a habit. I had smoked it for more than twenty years for medical purposes only, and I didn't have to smoke it after July. After Mr. Emmet heard my story, he didn't cancel our partnership.

I worked for Mr. Paul Emmet for almost twenty years. In 1957 I had been away from my village for more than thirty-seven years. I had reached the age of sixty and was still a bachelor. I returned to Hong Kong and got married. The next year my wife came to join me. I stayed in Courtland for one more year. During this time my boss and his wife passed away and the orchard was sold. Some people still asked me to farm for them but I decided to retire and move my family to Locke. Now I have two daughters and one son, all of whom are attending college. This is in 1980, and it has been almost sixty years that I have lived in the Delta.

Lum Bunn Fong (1893-1958)

The family of Lum Bunn Fong is one of the several Chinese families that continues to farm in the Delta along the Sacramento River. Although Lum Bunn Fong himself is dead, his three sons continue in the farming business he founded. The farm headquarters is located on Race Track Road, Walnut Grove. (Walnut Grove is just across a slough from Locke.)

The story of Lum Bunn Fong was told by his former foreman/bookkeeper, Joy Low. Joy Low explained that, trusted by his ranch hands and admired by outsiders for his courteous and straightforward manner, Lum Bunn Fong was hard-working and thrifty. He possessed a keen business sense which eventually enabled him to purchase nearly 400 acres of good farmland in the Delta, land farmed today by his children.

Lum Bunn Fong probably came from China, entering the United States as a "paper son" when he was very young. Some people, however, say that he was born in San Francisco in 1893. His family was part of the San Francisco Chinatown scene until 1906 when the earthquake and fire destroyed it. The Fong family moved to Sacramento in 1906 and Lum Bunn spent several of his teen years there. Then he went to Courtland in the Delta and worked there until 1911.

Lum Bunn struggled and worked very hard. He worked for others until he was able to lease land to farm by himself. In the Depression, no one would even let him buy food on credit and at a certain point his electricity was even cut off because he

lacked ready cash. Times improved however, and in 1939, Lum Bunn bought his home ranch of 196 acres, thereby becoming the most extensive Chinese landowner in the Delta. The ranch he bought was growing sugar beets and there were only twenty to thirty acres of rather small pears. In 1941, he added 201 acres to his holdings. Besides his own land, Lum Bunn rented hundreds of additional acres, and thus kept his men and machinery working. He grew sugar beets, corn, and pears, and usually made a good profit. His main crew consisted of about ten men who lived on the ranch. During the growing season, however, he employed more than seventy workers. All of his workers were Chinese.

Chinese do not usually believe in someone, but if they do, they believe in him completely. About twenty or thirty of the men employed by Lum Bunn trusted him so much that they deposited most or all of their salary into Lum Bunn's account, and considered him as their bank. The workers only received $1.75 a day (at that time, milk was only ten cents a bottle and bread was only ten cents a loaf; besides, Lum Bunn provided room and board). But in thirty days this came to $52.50, and multiplied times twenty to thirty workers, it came to $1050-$1575 a month.

Those workers who wanted to send money back to their families in China or send any goods back to their homes had to mail it themselves; this was a management rule of Lum Bunn Fong. Lum Bunn also asked Joy Low, as his foreman/bookkeeper, to write letters for those who could not write. If a letter arrived for a worker and if he wanted Joy to read it for him, Joy did so. Joy also oversaw the workers. He recorded their schedules and their work hours and took care of payday, which came on Sundays. He kept records of those who wanted their paychecks, and also a record of those who did not want their paychecks that month; he kept the record of the money that workers deposited into Lum Bunn's own bank account. As the foreman/bookkeeper Joy Low had a little more freedom that the other workers and at the end of the year, he received a bonus (*fa-hung*) from Lum Bunn.

Lum Bunn brought his wife to California in 1929 and they had six children. He loved all his children. He was successful in business, but he wanted his children to have a good education and to learn to appreciate the value of hard work. He also wanted them to continue his enterprise. His three sons graduated from college. The eldest son majored in management, and also became familiar with the mechanical work of the new farm equipment. The second son graduated from the University of California at Davis and majored in agriculture. Now his three sons have divided their responsibilities. The eldest son is in charge of all mechanical and farm equipment; the second son takes care of crops (planting, fertilizing, etc.) and the third son is in charge of the laborers (hiring, work schedules, and the like).

When he died at the age of sixty-five, Lum Bunn Fong left shares of his land

and business to his three daughters as well as to his sons. The sons bought back the operating shares from their sisters. (The sisters still have shares of the property.) This made it easier to accomplish things. Otherwise, there would have been too many bosses to handle the family farming business. The business was then incorporated as "Lum Bunn Sons."

Joe Young, who also worked for Lum Bunn, recalls that Lum Bunn was a very nice person and taught him a lot about farming. Joe Young appreciated the fact that Lum Bunn did not mind taking the time to teach Joe and others pruning and packing jobs, and the right way to cultivate fruit trees. Lum Bunn ignored other's complaints about spending too much time teaching young workers how to work.

Chapter 7

Growing Up in the Delta
(Alfred Jung and Jack Chew)

Alfred Jung (1917-1983)

My parents were born in Chungshan, China and they came to the United States in 1901. They mainly worked in a tailor shop but also had other kinds of businesses in San Francisco. My sister was born in 1904. I was born in 1917 in San Francisco. My sister got married in 1922 when she was eighteen years old. After she married she moved to Courtland and lived with her husband. At that time I was only five years old and I went to live with them.

My brother-in-law's name was Lai Foon and he was about twenty-eight years old when he married my sister. He was a farmer working in the Courtland area. The orchard where he worked is located at the "River Mansion" on Grant Island where people hold big parties every year. My sister, her husband and I lived in a farmhouse on that ranch. The farmhouse was built by the ranch owner and there was a large dining room which could hold over thirty people during dinner. My sister worked in the kitchen preparing meals for the laborers. My brother-in-law worked on the farm. He also hired and supervised laborers for pruning and harvesting.

I went to kindergarten in Courtland, and I usually took the school bus to school. Occasionally, if I missed the school-bus, I would be picked up by Lily Chow who at one time went to the same school. Lily Chow (whose married name is Lily Chen) was the daughter of our neighbor, Mr. Chow Yu-Kwan, who farmed a small ranch. After staying one year with my sister, my parents took me back to San Francisco, but periodically I came back to visit my sister.

A few years later, in 1929, my sister and her husband quit farming and moved to Locke. They lived on Third Street. At this time I returned to Locke and lived with my sister again. Locke was then a very busy and lively Chinese town, particularly during harvest seasons. There were many people gathered around the town. As for me, I attended Walnut Grove Grammar School where I met many friends. Our main recreation as young kids was dancing, playing the guitar and playing **ma jong**. In fact, our school had dancing parties once in awhile and we always liked to go. At that time the dances were mostly slow. Sometimes we went to Sacramento to see a movie. It

was easy for us to get a ride to Sacramento because very frequently Yuen Chong Market's employees needed to go to Sacramento to do some buying for the market; it was no problem for us to go with them. We also liked to go fishing and swimming along the river near the Locke pier.

In the summer of my twelfth year I started to work for a farmer, Wong Chung-Kau. He was a good friend of my uncle Chan Kum (a shopowner), so I got a chance to work on his ranch. My job was sorting pears. On that ranch sorting pears was primarily done by women, old men and youngsters like me. There were six to eight workers in the packing department, with the same Chinese workers being hired back every year to pack the fruit. These workers were very experienced in the process so they worked very fast. Although there were machines to help, most of the work was still done by hand. The ranch had its own shed and pier on the riverbank. The shed was used as its packing department, and there were railroad tracks connecting the packing place to the ranch.

Before the harvest season started and the packing began, the workers in the packing department had to do some preparatory work such as making and labelling the shipping boxes. After the fruit was harvested on the ranch it was transported to the packing shed by trucks or horsecarts. Then, workers put the fruit into a machine which had a long conveyor belt in it. The machine washed the fruit and moved it to the belt then transported it to a disc for sorting. Several workers stood beside the belt and picked out the bad ones, leaving the good fruit to the sorting process. The fruit then went through a separating disc and was sorted in to large, medium and small sizes. Then it was ready for packing in boxes. We worked from 6 a.m. to 6 p.m. Sometimes we worked overtime.

Not all ranches had their own packing shed and pier. Those ranches that did not have their own packing facilities would let a specialized packing company manage their fruit. My sister worked in one of these big companies. She was a forewoman in the fruit packing process. Some Chinese people called her by her maiden name, Jung Sui Ngo and some called her by her married name, Mrs. Lai Foon. At that time she was quite a well-known person among the Chinese ladies. My sister spoke English and Chinese. She always helped the Chinese to communicate with the Americans. Many Chinese relied on her for an interpreter. When people went to see their doctor they would ask her to interpret for them. Her husband, Lai Foon, knew only a little English and so she really helped him in his farming and other businesses. At one time they also operated a restaurant on Main Street in Locke. Later, she and her husband moved to Los Angeles.

When I started working for Wong Chung-Kau, he was only in his forties and he had a very large ranch. Besides farming he had to take care of his laborers' room and board, and so he had hired a cook. I remember the cook, So Yung Ng, whose

cooking was delicious! I lived in Locke for two years until I graduated from elementary school.* Then I went back to San Francisco and continued high school. During my high school years in San Francisco, however, I went back to the Delta on my summer vacations every year and most of the summers I worked at Chung-Kau's ranch.

As I got older I no longer worked in the packing department, but instead I worked in the fields picking fruit [pears]. It was a tough job. I had to take the heavy wooden ladders to the field by myself. Every morning at 6 a.m. after I had breakfast I went out to the field with a group of three or four people. Every one of us carried a bucket, then we climbed up the ladder and picked the fruit. We were instructed to pick only the ripe ones and those that were about the same size. Therefore, we could not pick many fruit at one time in one spot. We had to get down and move the ladder to another spot of the tree and go up to do the same thing again and again. Because the ladder was very heavy and was one of the 'A' shape kind, it could not be folded. It was at least twelve feet long and we had to be very careful in moving it from one spot to another spot. Otherwise, we could easily fall. After we got a bucketful of fruit we unloaded it into a box. When the box was full a horsecart would come to take the fruit away. The weather was very hot, especially in the afternoon. We had two breaks, besides the lunch hour. One break was at 9 a.m. and the other break was at 3 p.m.

I lived on Chung-Kau's ranch while I worked there during the summers. As I recall I lived in a two-story building. The second floor was used for our resting and sleeping area and the ground floor was used for the dining room. During work days we usually stayed in this house at the ranch in the evenings, reading newspapers or talking to each other. We went to bed very early, around 8 p.m., and we fell asleep very easily. You could hear the people snoring very loudly. During the weekends some workers went to Locke. I was the youngest of all the workers.

I recall there was one summer that I worked for Wong Chung-Kau's cousin, Wong Chung-Fat. He assigned me to pull grass in an asparagus field. As far as I can remember, not many people worked on this grass pulling job. I worked continuously under the summer heat, bending down pulling grass throughout the day. I felt that was too tough for me, so after working for three days I quit that job.

There was one summer that I worked in a dry good store in Walnut Grove. The store owner was a Mr. Lai. Besides taking care of the regular customers, I was asked by Mr. Lai to collect Chinese lottery tickets [Chinese keno, also called **pak-kop piu**] at the store. The Chinese lottery tickets were almost like regular keno tickets at casi-

---

*In those days, elementary school included grades one through eight.

nos in Reno and Lake Tahoe. Instead of using numbers from one to eighty, however, eighty different Chinese characters were used.* I marked the tickets for the players. I learned eighty extra Chinese words by doing this. The players were mostly farm workers and all were Chinese. At that time many Chinese stores set up this practice as a side business. They formed a network for the main lottery and gambling house. The stores sold and collected the lottery tickets but the lottery was operated by the gambling house. People did not have to go to the gambling house in order to play the game. There were only two games a day. I heard that many stores participated in this network. It only operated during the summer when there were lots of Chinese in towns like Locke and Walnut Grove.

Chinese college students from San Francisco also worked in the orchards. These students did not necessarily need to know any friends or relatives here in order to get a job here. Some returned to work for several summers. Some came because their friends had come to get a job here. It became a tradition for Chinese college students to work on a ranch. Perhaps it was because they found the environment different from the city: It was like a combination of making money, going on vacation and camping at the ranch. When I look back at those summer days, it was fun, but I cannot say it was an easy life.

Other interesting events that I can remember in the past concern the night watchman, Ban Bing. I did not know his surname. I just called him Uncle Ban Bing. He was not my real uncle but it was the Chinese custom to address someone who was older as 'uncle'. In those days when I went to Locke I took the ship from San Francisco. The ship made several stops before arriving at Locke and it would continue its trip to Courtland and Sacramento. I always took the 6 p.m. ride from San Francisco. When it arrived at Locke, it was about 1 a.m. Uncle Ban Bing usually came and took me to my uncle's store. As the night watchman he guarded the town of Locke. Maybe he was hired by the businessmen as a security guard. His job was to walk around the town during the night. He carried a wooden block and a stick. He was supposed to strike the block gently as he walked along. His other duty was to tell time at night. When it was 1 a.m. he stopped and struck the block once (with a loud sound). When it was two o'clock he struck twice (with a loud sound) and so on until five o'clock. I heard there were people who did the same thing in villages in China. It was interesting that in the early days this same practice was found in this Chinese town of Locke in California.

Jack Chew

I was born on October 9, 1909 in Courtland, and was one of several brothers

---

*The game keno as played in Reno, Lake Tahoe, etc. actually comes from this Chinese lottery.

and sisters. I was the eldest boy in the family. I went to Chinese school in Courtland which I attended every week night from 5:00 p.m. to 9:00 p.m. and on Saturday mornings. Schooling came easily to me. In fact, I was one of the top students in the Chinese school, as well as in the American school. Because of my constant association with my grandmother, I easily mastered the Chinese lessons, and quickly comprehended the exact meanings of words. Even now, although I can't write many Chinese words, I can recognize them and can still read Chinese. In the late 1940s when I became a monitor in the United States State Department, I had a brief refresher course in Chinese because it was necessary for me to relearn the language for my job. Now I have been retired for many years and have again lost most of my knowledge of written Chinese.

In Courtland there was a public school for Orientals and a public school for white children, both of which had been in existence long before I attended. The former was established because the Oriental population (Japanese and Chinese) was a substantial portion of the entire community. I went through all the primary grades in the Oriental school, but I went to a high school where Chinese and whites were integrated. I graduated from Courtland High School, and can still remember some of my classmates, some of whom are still living, such as Tim Cheng, Bob Jang, and Norman Cheng.

When I was young, I remember some older boys fought with white boys. They didn't fight in school but outside of it. In the Delta area there were few actual fights but in San Francisco there were many confrontations between Chinese and Italians. Chinese, for example, couldn't go to the Italian part of town and Italians couldn't come to the Chinese section. But in the Delta the clashes were few because in grammar school the two factions were separated and didn't come into contact with each other. When the children went home, they were also out of touch with each other. The only time Chinese and whites associated while I was in grammar school was when they played ball at an inter-school sports activity. Their parents and many friends came to watch the games. There were quite a few American-born Chinese who also liked to watch. After I got to high school I was on the same team with white players. There still weren't many racial problems of which anyone was aware. Challenging discrimination hadn't come into fashion yet. I remember that many whites came to Courtland's Chinatown for entertainment and didn't discriminate against the Chinese. Most were farmers and their children from the Delta. Although the cities had racial problems, the rural areas had few incidents. In the country the distance between houses was so great that people didn't often run into each other. If that kind of conflict ever existed, it was very minor.

I enjoyed high school life very much, and made all the first teams in sports. My academic life was good because the teachers liked me, and I made the honor roll every month. I got along well with my white peers and attribute this to my parents. I feel

59

that I integrated more readily because I used to go to their [white friends] homes and stay overnight. I mingled with whites more than any other Chinese at that time and even dated [white] American girls in high school.

I went to the University of California, Berkeley where I studied electrical engineering. However, I did not graduate because I saw that there would be no job opportunities for me in this field in those days. All of my brothers and sisters also went to college.

When I left the Delta in 1928, I went to college but during the summer I returned to the ranch to help. After a couple of years of college I worked for Joe Shoong in his Dollar Store chain* starting in San Francisco then moving to Salinas, Modesto, Long Beach, Los Angeles, Seattle, Portland and other places. I felt very close to the Shoong family. Joe Shoong had grown up in Sacramento, and my father had known him well. Joe was always in the merchandise business and was very clever at it, eventually expanding his original business in Sacramento to San Francisco and other cities. During the Depression he hired many Chinese to work in his chain of sixty stores.

In 1940 I became so sick that I had to be admitted to a hospital. After recuperating I returned to Courtland, fixed up the family house, and lived there for about five years. While I was in Courtland the Japanese relocation began so I returned to farming. Since my father hadn't bought any land in the Delta area I spent three years leasing land. I took over three of the Japanese ranches when their owners were forced into relocation camps by the United States government. A good friend, Leong Kwan-Luk, helped me during this time.

During the time that I farmed the price of the crops was totally dependent on the canneries which fixed the prices. If they didn't want my produce, they wouldn't even make me an offer. I didn't feel right about that so I quit. In 1946 I moved to Sacramento and started my own business.

While I was in Courtland, the State Department wanted someone to help them with immigration problems. My father, Chancy Chew, had attended St. Joseph's Academy with a man who later became director of the immigration office in San Francisco, and the immigration director wanted to get his help since he knew the Delta area. However, my father had died in 1937. So the immigration office director came to Courtland and asked me to work for the department. In talking to the man, I learned that the immigration office wanted to adjust the status of all the Chinese in the Delta. There were about 1,300 Chinese whose status had to be cleared up. So I promised

---

*Joe Shoong, founder and owner of the Dollar Stores, was at his death the wealthiest Chinese living in the United States. He engaged in philanthropy and especially liked to donate money to Chinese schools.

60

to work with the immigration officials on the condition that when the status of each Chinese in question was clarified, prosecution would not occur. Instead, the officials would let the people readjust their status. The agreement was made, and as an employee of the State Justice Department I helped close the file on 3,000 cases concerning Delta Chinese. The difficulty of this work can be seen from an example. One woman had over 1,000 children according to bogus papers and birth certificates and they were all sons! The cases had been extended from father to grandfather and so on, becoming endlessly convoluted.

Eventually, Officials discovered that an American lawyer and a Chinese had manufactured all the fraudulent papers. They charged an average of $350 for their services, the attorney receiving $250, his Chinese partner, $100. But the Chinese confederate sold his share for more profit — sometimes as much as $1,000. The two men used the same woman in the same city as the mother of all these "paper sons." These two men eventually were arrested and prosecuted. I had studied law for two years at Golden Gate College while working for Joe Shoong, and I was able to introduce four or five men as witnesses for the State in the prosecution of the two men. In return for this service, the Chinese in the Delta area had their status readjusted.

My father and grandfather also lived in the Delta. Everything that I know about my grandfather I learned from other people, since my grandfather died before I was born.

My grandfather was commonly called "Ah-Chew," and most American people addressed him as Mr. Chew. His surname was Lum. He came to California around 1854 when he was about fifteen years old (about seventeen, by Chinese reckoning), with many people of similar age. He originally went to work in the gold mines, but gold mining was such that common practice and the attitude of the other miners made it very difficult for Chinese miners to earn a living. For this reason, he left the gold fields and came to the Delta to look for work. In addition to work as farm laborer, around 1870 the building of levees provided another source of employment, and attracted many Chinese from the gold mining country. Of course, levee building was very hard work, but at least it was steady. Work camps moved south as the levee construction progressed. The laborers stopped at the little town of Hood, then at Courtland. At Mr. Deming's invitation my grandfather started working on his ranch.

After my grandfather had decided to settle down in the Sacramento Delta, he went back to China on a sailboat to marry, and then brought his wife over here. My grandfather's first home was in Hood. The Chinese had built two houses there at that time and my grandfather was living in part of one of them when my grandmother first arrived in America. He was employed in an orchard on a seasonal basis, working as a crew member whenever the farmers needed him. Invariably, however, he would also work for Mr. Deming on the latter's Courtland ranch.

My grandfather was evidently a very likeable fellow who was on good terms with Mr. and Mrs. Deming and their family. The Demings even made a verbal contract with my father that he and his family could stay on their ranch as long as the Demings were alive. The relationship between the Demings and the Chews was very close, and I was born on the ranch.

My grandfather had three sons, and all three were born in the house in Courtland. When the eldest son was born, Mrs. Deming named him "Chancy," a very British name because she was British. But instead of simply calling him Chancy Chew his parents inserted "Lum" (the family's Chinese surname) between the "Chancy" and the "Chew," to end up with Chancy Lum Chew. Chancy Lum Chew was my father.

Mrs. Deming was quite concerned about my father's English education. In the Delta at that time schooling was difficult. There was no school where the Chews lived so my father, Chancy, was sent to a semiprivate school called the St. Joseph Academy in Rio Vista where he received a formal English education. He graduated from there with the equivalent of a high school education. Then he came back to the farm on the Deming ranch. He had no formal Chinese education, but he was able to speak the language fluently. In 1905, he married Sharon Wong in San Francisco.

My father farmed on Mr. Deming's ranch, working as a tenant farmer under the share crop system and doing other work as well. In the Delta at that time few Chinese, with the exception of my father, were fluent in English. Being able to speak both English and Chinese, my father was frequently consulted by white landowners and asked to furnish Chinese laborers for different kinds of crops, such as hops and vineyards. He was also asked to farm new crops and was a pioneer in many ways. With several other Chinese partners in a large and difficult venture he raised onions, potatoes and other vegetables on an island which had never before been cultivated. The enormity of the operation necessitated his buying large tractors and other sophisticated farm equipment. After three or four years, however, the area's farming industry as a whole went through a slump, forcing my father and his partners to sell out. My father turned his misfortune to advantage. In 1915, getting away from farming, he went into a labor contracting business. He furnished laborers for hop ranches, dry yards, grape vineyards, apricot ranches, and the like. Many farmers patronized him, since it was easy for him to gather a group of thirty to forty Chinese on short notice to work at harvesting, cultivating, pruning and the like. Furthermore, my father had his own truck to transport the workers and this made his services even more sought after.

After he became a labor contractor, my father moved from the Deming ranch to Courtland (about a quarter of a mile away), while his brother remained on the ranch. In Courtland, he built a home where the whole family could live. In town he was engaged in other businesses as well as labor contracting. He opened a general

merchandise store and an ice cream shop. He also went into partnership in a restaurant, and invested in gambling houses in town. Courtland had a fairly large and successful Chinese community at that time, composed primarily of people from Chungshan County. The community flourished until part of the town was damaged by a fire, after which most of the Chinese left for San Francisco [sic].

In 1927 my father started a summer school in Courtland for children whose parents wanted them to learn Chinese. He built a fence around his own house to lay out an area for the school. The students used the electricity from the house and had tables and chairs in the yard. There were about ten students. My father hired the teacher, although the children did have to pay a monthly tuition to help with the teacher's salary. The school lasted about three years. Later, the Chinese community in Courtland started its own school along the same lines.

Dr. Sun Yat-Sen, the Chinese revolutionary hero, visited the Sacramento Delta several times before 1911 — he died in 1925. His visits to the Delta greatly affected the Chinese communities there. The Chinese Nationalist Party [Kuomintang, or KMT] became quite powerful because of Sun Yat-sen's visits, particularly in Courtland. My father was one of those who became active in Sun Yat-sen's movement to change China. He spent a great deal of money for this cause. He was the buying agent for Sun Yat-sen's air force and used the back of a ranch where there were no trees as a training area for pilots. My father bought some planes left over from World War I from the Janson Company. Besides the expense of the aircraft, he also donated money to Sun Yat-sen's group.

The flyers were young Chinese men from Courtland, Honolulu, Seattle and Portland. They went to some other town where they received their initial training, and then they came to Courtland and tested out guns on the ranch. They also flew the planes every time one was available. An American named Edward was the teacher. He completed the men's flight training by teaching them to fly, to repair planes, to disassemble them, and so forth. They trained on the ranch for several months, living in camps set up there for them. My father stored the planes and kept them ready for shipment when they would be needed. He was waiting for the command to transport them, but the planes never reached China because someone set a fire, (around 1929/30) purposely destroying them all. This was the first time I ever saw my father cry. The fire itself was reported in the local newspaper but the Chinese never revealed what was inside the storage house that had been destroyed.

Chapter 8
Wives, Gambling Days, and Retirement in Locke
(Mrs. Jong Ho Leong, Mrs. Joe Chow, Steven Chan, Hoy Kee)

Mrs. Jong Ho Leong

I have lived in Locke since the 1940s. I was born on January 1, 1905, at Tai Wan Village, Chungshan, China, and studied for four years at a Christian school. I deeply believed in the Bible, although I was not baptized, and thought that all religions basically teach people to be good. I did not learn very much English in school.

My father was a merchant who worked in Europe. My grandfather was the County Supervisor and later became the Ambassador to Cuba. I was a traditional Chinese woman from a middle income family. My marriage was arranged by my parents, which was the custom in those days. I was sixteen years old then and did not really know my husband beforehand. My husband, whose real Chinese name was Lai, was living in the United States, and he went back to China to marry me. We lived happily together in Chungshan County for quite awhile, and bought some land and started farming. Then my husband came back to the United States and began working in the Delta. In 1940, because of World War II, I sold my farm in China and moved to Locke to join my husband. At that time there were already shops, grocery stores and restaurants in Locke. There were many Chinese people living and working in Locke and children were going to school. My own two sons were born in Lodi. A doctor came to Locke from Lodi and drove me back to Lodi and delivered my children. I rested for four days and then had to go back to Locke and begin working again. By then, my husband and I were working very hard.

At that time, many Chinese were working for an asparagus packing company. Our packing job consisted of tying asparagus into bundles and then packing them into packages. Sometimes we did some transporting work such as moving the packages of asparagus to a nearby pier for shipping. If a large amount of asparagus came into town, we would have to wake up at 5 a.m. and begin working. If the amount of asparagus was not very much on a particular day, we began working in the afternoon. Our job was to pack all the asparagus that was provided for that day. So, there were times when we worked into the evenings to finish the job. Usually, February and March were the two busiest working months. In April, we stopped working in

the packing company and went to work in the cannery in Isleton. Not only did the men and women in Locke work, but some of the children also began working at the age of eleven or twelve. These children usually came home from school at 4 p.m. and went to work to help their parents. My husband and I usually worked for the cannery until the end of September. Besides this work, we had other odd jobs, such as packing prunes and other kinds of fruit at $1.75 a day. During November and December, we also did some farming, like growing onions and garlic.

The cannery mostly employed Chinese women.* When women needed to go to work during the day, they could leave their little children in a special kindergarten which belonged to the canning company. There were babysitters who took care of the young ones, and the employees did not have to pay for this service. The company also provided housing for all the employees. The rent for the dormitories was only $2 a week, and the amount was returned to the employee if he or she worked for a complete period (usually one year) in the factory. Unfortunately, for one reason or other, the company closed down, and this affected mostly the Chinese workers in Locke. Therefore, these workers had to go to Sacramento for jobs, but due to their poor English, they found it very hard to communicate with the Americans. This, of course, made it difficult for them to be employed.

While working in the cannery, my husband's arm was cut off by the canning machine in an accident. After he came out of the hospital, he could not continue to work. The insurance company claimed that it was his fault and did not pay him any insurance. Therefore, he could only receive welfare funds from the government. After this time, I was the only one who took care of and supported the whole family. I worked at almost all kinds of jobs and worked very hard to raise my two sons. Then my husband passed away. It was the saddest period of my life, but I had courage and came through all right and things started to get better for me. In 1969 my two sons went to college and I was proud of the fact that they graduated and now have good jobs. I retired at the age of sixty-two and I now have a calm, peaceful and simple life in Locke.

Now, my grandchildren are grown up too (I have four granddaughters: fifteen, fourteen, thirteen, and eleven years old; one grandson). They are very clever and nice to me. All the grandchildren are from my younger son. My elder son hasn't married yet. A lot of people came to me and asked about my son (for marriage), including cousins, people from our village in China, and so on, but my son said he would rather decide that himself.

---

*This cannery was owned by Thomas Foon Chew, a Chinese American. It normally employed Chinese-speaking people as supervisors, and was particularly concerned about the Chinese who worked for the company.

66

I like to recall those memories of my younger days as a farm laborer. Once I had to work very late during January to finish planting onions in the field. Since it was very cold and foggy, some of the workers burned firewood to keep warm, and one of the workers stood too close with his back to the fire and caught fire. He wasn't really hurt, and it was very funny.

I was happy that the government restored my house and provided me with a new heater. Although my son has a much larger house, I would still rather live alone in Locke. Locke is exactly like the village we lived in while in China. Everybody knows each other and works together. We survived only because we helped each other out.

Mrs. Joe Chow (1897-1980)

My husband was Owyang Hong Kerng and my maiden name is Ho Lan Ching, but my English name is Mrs. Joe Chow. My husband was born in Dai Leung, Chungshan County, China. I was born in Chong Ga Bin Village, about three miles from the county seat, Shek Kei. My husband came to the United States when he was ten years old. He was the youngest of three brothers. They all came here and worked and died, but their children are all in San Francisco and Sacramento. My husband passed away about ten years ago when he was about ninety years old. Now, I am eighty-two and I have forgotten most of my husband's life stories. However, I know that he went back to China several times and he married me on one of his trips back to China. When I married him, I was about sixteen. In those days, if a girl did not get married by eighteen, she was teased as being an old maid, therefore, it was common practice to get married at an early age. After we got married, he came back to the United States.

Before I got married in China, my grandmother would not allow me or other girls to go to school. She argued that it was useless for girls to go to school. Instead, I learned how to cook and to work in the rice fields. I came to the United States in the 1930s because the war with Japan had broken out in China. At that time my husband was a farmer, so I helped him and worked in the orchards. Later since we lost money, we stopped farming and my husband worked as a laborer and I worked in the canneries. There I canned tomatoes, asparagus and peaches. I used to work more than ten hours for $2.50 a day. I also worked at the pier in the packing house, weighing and packing fresh asparagus. My rate of pay was one cent for each pack of asparagus. Dozens of people crammed in the packing house. It was very crowded and everyone kept very busy. Sometimes we worked in the evenings too.

I have two sons, two daughters and ten grandchildren who live in San Francisco and Sacramento. I live here in Locke alone, but I have many friends in the town.

Steven Chan

I was born in 1903 in Tung Houh Village, Chungshan County, China. I lived in my childhood and youth in Hong Kong. My parents were well educated and my grandfather was wealthy so I was able to concentrate on my studies. It was not necessary for me to work. My father was working in the United States police station as a translator (English to Chinese) while I was still a student in Hong Kong. My grandfather and uncles had come to America in the early 1900s.

In 1918 when I was fifteen years old, I came to America with my people from my village. I had planned to become a tailor at my parents' fashion shop, but I was drafted because of World War I. After I came back from the war, I opened my own tailor shop (located on Geary Street in San Francisco). In this shop I made only women's custom fashions in dresses and shirts. I even hired a few salesmen to take orders. Business was not good, however, so eventually I had to close my shop. It was at the time when many businesses were being closed.

After I closed my business, I moved to Locke, although I had never worked on a farm before. I was not the healthy outdoor type. After arriving in Locke, I simply relaxed and spent my time fishing. Eventually I began working in a canning factory. After working at this job for awhile, I went back to China to get married. After I arrived, my village people introduced me to my wife. Later, I found out that my father-in-law had been in the United States for many years. In fact, I became acquainted with him after my marriage, although I think I had met him in Locke around 1920. In the 1920s I went to Locke frequently and the town was very lively.

In 1945, I went back to Locke to look around for a job, but I still could not find anything suitable because I was not well educated in the United States and I could not work on a farm. For these reasons, I ended up working in a gambling house. I did not know the first thing about gambling houses so I was taught that my job was to simply sit and play as a dummy player. At this job, I made only about $20 a week. What I earned then was enough to keep me living so I could not ask for anything more. Furthermore, the job was only temporary, so whenever I was out of work, I went fishing. Many people came to gamble at the house including Filipinos, Americans, Chinese and Japanese. I worked at the gambling house for one and a half years, until the gambling houses in Locke began to be closed down by the attorney general. At first little towns like Locke were not controlled by the law. Later however, even small towns came to be controlled by the law.

After I quit working in the gambling house, some friends of mine introduced me to work in the cannery. I worked for another two years on this job and saved some money. Then I had my family brought to the United States (around 1947) and found a place to settle down. After I had my two children I bought this house in Locke; it had been a bar before, and was built in 1912. I bought this house in 1950

when most of the bars were already closed down. Most of the houses around Locke were built by the Chinese, but my house was built by Americans. When I chose this house I did not care about its outside appearance. I only cared about its inside appearance. There was a large refrigerator in the kitchen when I bought the house, but since then it has been removed. I have been living in this house for over thirty years. I do not need to pay taxes on this house because I am a veteran.

None of my children know much Chinese because they did not have a chance to learn it. (Their high schools did not offer Chinese). I was a secretary in Locke's Chun Ying Association for almost twenty years. I did Chinese calligraphy, too, and I was often asked by some of my friends for my calligraphy. Now, I am old; I do not care about things such as this. I remember in the olden days when I was in Locke, people would ask for my help and I always liked helping them.

All my four children were born in Locke. When they were born, I was still working in the cannery. My wages were low and life was rough. But fortunately, things were priced reasonably in those days and I was quite thrifty. When my eldest son was twelve years old, he had a newspaper route, delivering the *Sacramento Bee*. He made about 50ᶜ a day. Since it rained most of the time during the winter, I usually used my car to help him out because he was unable to ride his bicycle. That would cost me about $1 a day, and it rained very frequently. Sometimes it rained for a whole week. I remember one time, my son woke up at four in the morning and said to me, "It is raining, I want to quit delivering the newspaper." Then I told him, "Son, keep on the job. That is your duty. Do not give up on anything you do. You must be consistent with your work." Now, my eldest son is thirty-four years old. That is the reason why he is now working with the government, and he has been working on the job for more than ten years. If you do not care about your children or teach them when they are young, especially the Chinese children who grow up in the United States, when they get older, they will not listen to you anymore. You have to train them and let them know about their parents' past experiences, then they will learn to work harder themselves. During the summer, all my children would work in the packing houses to earn money for school. Even though all of them had scholarships for their studies, it was certainly not enough to cover all their expenses, therefore, they needed to work during the summer.

Some parents like to buy toys for their children, but I bought books for them to read. In fact, I bought a lot of books and magazines in the old days, and I have saved them all. Since I was not well educated in the United States, all I could do was buy books for them and hope that they could learn from the books. I bought them an encyclopedia, so that if they had anything that they did not understand, they could look it up themselves.

Nowadays, our society does not talk about literature. It only cares about science and technology. In the old days, Chinese literature and language were stressed. That is why sometimes when I write in modern Chinese, I have to use the classical Chinese poetry model to help me in presenting my thoughts. In the old times when I was still young, I liked to write poems, and I mailed them to newspapers. In fact, I wrote three poems that the *Chinese Times* in San Francisco accepted and printed using my name "Steven Chan, Locke." During this time, writing was only my hobby, but now I realize I was not a good writer then. I feel sorry for taking the space in the newspaper. There is a Chinese proverb that you only will find that books (knowledge) are not enough when you really need to use them. [i.e., you can never learn enough]. At any rate, I have continued writing poems from time to time, but I did not have them printed in a newspaper. Sometimes I have enjoyed expressing myself in poems to please myself. Mainly, I have written poems when someone has asked me to do so.

I remember the year when my son and daughter both graduated from high school. I wrote the following poem for them!

Through seventy-two years of struggles, the man is now alone, A foreigner in this foreign country which time has made his home.
His future will flow by like the water, just as has the past;
His heart has cooled and the flame does not last.
He cares not for his passing, nor bemoans yellow leaves in the fall
But knows winter flowers will not flourish, need strive no more.
There is one thing which pleases him — his children have worked hard
Getting their degrees, and bring love to his heart.

October 31, 1980
(translated from Chinese)

Hoy Kee (1894-1984)

My father worked as a farm laborer in Hawaii and died there before I came to the United States. He was nice enough to send me to school in China to learn to read and write Chinese. Although I studied for just two or three years, I was considered fortunate. I did not learn very much at that time because I was young. When I got older I went to Hong Kong. I did nothing except tour the various places in Hong Kong. Finally, in 1915 I came to the United States with my friends.

After entering the United States, I stayed at Angel Island for a whole month. Some of my companions had to stay there for half a year. Fortunately, my relatives came for me when I was at Angel Island. While I was there I did not experience the unkind treatment that many Chinese did. The immigration officer did not ask me too many questions.

Most of the Chinese in Locke, including me, originally came from Chungshan County, although there were some who came from Sze Yap. After living in Locke, I went to Orchard Ranch and worked at an American farm for seven years. I was married, but I left my family behind when I first came to the United States. In 1922 I went back to China and visited my wife. She later moved to Macao and died there. At that time nobody brought their wife with them to the United States.

On my way back to China the first time, I also visited Hawaii for more than ten days. After my first trip back to China, I worked in a casino in Reno for awhile and later came back to work at a gambling hall in Locke. The gambling hall that I worked in was owned by Sze Yap people. They were nice and I liked them. There are still some Sze Yap people in Walnut Grove. Gambling was popular. There were three gambling places in Walnut Grove and two in Locke.

Approximately 100-200 Filipinos came to Walnut Grove in the 1920s. Now there are only about ten Filipinos there. Most of the gamblers were Filipinos at that time. Some Japanese and Americans also gambled there. It was better to serve Japanese than Americans because the Japanese gave us more tips when they won. The basic unit of money for gambling was a quarter at that time. The gambling places were open from 10 a.m. to 10 p.m. The workers could take one hour breaks after working for two hours. There were two free meals and coffee was served in the morning. I earned at least $2 plus tips a day. Although the owner seemed to give us a generous wage, he still made far more than we did.

I do not know who started the gambling business there. I know that Charlie Bing Lee owned a gambling place. The ownership of the other gambling halls changed quite often. There were also some Chinese ladies working at the gambling houses. Spancer Ow Yang, from San Francisco, was the interpreter between Charlie Bing Lee and the landowner, Mr. Locke. Spancer was born in Walnut Grove and he went to high school there. He worked at the Bank of America in San Francisco, then joined the Army. Spancer's father, who owned a business, lived here.

Ping Lee [the son of Charlie Bing Lee] is a friend of mine. Ping Lee's father had a market and he established the town. His father was a cook in an American restaurant. After he had made some money he built a house in Walnut Grove. Unfortunately, the house burned down, so he moved to Locke. Ping Lee is the owner of this building which was constructed by Americans. It was a gambling house before, but now it is a clubhouse called *The Happy Reading Club*, which was formed in 1975. Ping Lee is really nice and he allows us to read newspapers here. Since I retired at age sixty-five, I have been coming here to read and to meet people. In the mornings we often sit on the bench in front of the clubhouse. The club has about ten members and each of us contributes some money. Although we have not elected a president or other officers, we do have a bookkeeper.

The club subscribes to the *Chinese Times* from San Francisco. Our money also goes to pay for water, electricity, and so forth. We also organize two big banquets annually, although there is not a special occasion for the banquets. We have simple daily meals, but the banquets are fancy nine-course dinners. Mr. Chau Chow is a fine cook, and he drives to San Francisco to buy the best ingredients for cooking the nine-course dinners.

Conclusions: the Legacy

This book tells the story of Chinese in the Delta in the 20th century: their involvement in farming, their establishment of the town of Locke, and their more recent dispersal and retirement. It gives us a better idea of the breadth of the Chinese contribution, and helps correct exaggerated and sensationalized reports concerning opium smoking, gambling and prostitution in the Delta's Chinese communities.

The Chinese engaged in farming at a time in which the work had to be accomplished by manual labor rather than by machinery. In the face of great hardship, the Chinese did a marvelous job of cultivating the orchards and crop land. They helped establish many good farming practices which contributed to high yields. They understood what tasks they had to perform, and worked both diligently and conscientiously without supervision.

Chinese had a profound influence over the way commercial agriculture developed in California. In the mid-nineteenth century, Chinese set the pattern of contract labor which prevails even now: labor contractors recruit and manage a group of workers for landlords. The landlords only deal with the contractors, not with individual workers. Wages are often determined by the piece system instead of relying on hourly wages, and laborers leave when the job is over instead of incurring year-round expenses for the landlords. Contractors also can relinquish their obligations to their workers when the job is over. This system has greatly lowered production costs, especially in the nineteenth century, and has thereby contributed much to the success of California's agribusiness.

The Chinese also established California's system of farm tenancy under which several Chinese formed a partnership to lease land to farm. The tenant farmers paid an initial deposit and a percentage of the gross profits to the landlords. The landlords usually provided tools and shelter, and determined what kinds of crops would be grown. In addition, they were often responsible for pricing and marketing. The tenant farmers were in charge of all production and harvesting. This system has been workable and also provided a means whereby Chinese laborers in the Delta could improve their condition. The relationship between tenant farmers and landlords frequently involved mutual respect, and tenant farmers not only had more responsibility but could also make more money than a laborers.

Chinese in the Delta have indeed often been able to advance themselves. In 1860, most Chinese worked as farmhands, servants, and levee builders under white employers. From 1870 until at least 1890, however, most Chinese laborers were working for Chinese tenant farmers, and ever greater numbers of Chinese had become tenant farmers. Several elements appear to have been essential for a laborer to be-

come a tenant farmer: the laborer must have worked in the Delta for ten or even twenty years. In addition, some proficiency in English, a knowledge of general farm operations, a small amount of capital, good (Chinese) community contacts, and a willingness to take risk and responsibility were required. The three most common means by which a farm laborer could better himself socially and economically were to become a partner in a tenant farming partnership, to become a labor contractor, or to open a small business. Of course, not all laborers succeeded in advancing to one of these categories.

It has often been said that prior to 1949 Chinese immigrants returned most of their earnings to China. However, Chinese in the Delta did not send all their money home while they were working in the Delta or even when they retired and returned home to China. According to interviews, diaries and personal records, some of their savings remained in the United States in local banks or banks in San Francisco. Some laborers kept their money in their employers' accounts. Only a small portion of their savings were sent back to China, on a regular basis, the equivalent of twenty or twenty five percent of a laborer's earnings (which was enough to support a large number of family members in China). The Chinese who retired and returned to China did not take all their savings from the United States. Savings remained in American banks, or were placed in trust with friends or relatives in the United States. These practices amazed many American farmers.

Most of the retired farm laborers interviewed came to the United States when Chinese Exclusion was still in effect. Chinese immigrants were unwelcome. Many had forged immigration papers, and almost all had been interrogated at the notorious immigration station on Angel Island. These factors have made Chinese reluctant to talk about their feelings and their past with strangers; even with their own children. However, Chinese in the Delta feel that the treatment of Chinese immigrants and their children has been much better since the 1940s. They also feel that they have experienced less hostile treatment from whites than have Chinese who lived in the large cities. Fights and "tong wars" have also been much less acute in the Delta.

The experience of Chinese in the Delta — the farm laborers and tenant farmers, the inhabitants of Locke, the small businessmen, the wives, the gamblers — is a reminder of much of this country's immigrant past. Faced with serious obstacles, from a language barrier to a lack of capital, from racial antipathy to homesickness, they managed to secure for themselves a place in the New World. They settled in America, some permanently, some for decades, some for shorter periods of time. In spite of the tenuousness of their position, some even took up permanent residence in rural America, in the Delta. Many raised families. Almost all succeeded in contributing to the local economy and becoming an important part of California even while managing to improve their position and especially, their families' position. In spite of the hardships, they managed to fulfill a significant portion of the American dream while at the same time remaining true to their heritage.

74

Appendix:
Prompt Notes for a "Paper Son"

The following is a translation from some of the prompting notes used years ago by Wong Yow to help him enter this country as a "paper son." I have reorganized the notes to make reading easier.

Information about myself:

My surname is Wong, my given name Yow. I am from Heunghsan, [today's Chungshan County], Kwangtung, China. I was born in the village of Sek Ling in the district of Lung Dou. I am 19 years old now [all ages here are by Chinese reckoning]. I was born on August 8 in the 29th year of the Kuang-hsu Emperor [i.e., 1904].

My family:

My father's name is Wong Choi. He was born on May 29 in the 6th year of the Kuang-hsu Emperor (i.e., 1881). My mother's last name is Lau. She is 39 years old now and is a native of Kai Gok, a village about an hour's walk away from ours. My mother has a bound feet. I have a younger brother but no sisters. My brother's name is Wong Jau. He is 18 years old now and was born on October 20 in the 30th year of the Kuang-hsu Emperor (i.e., 1905). Neither my brother nor I are married yet. We have never been anywhere together before.

My relatives:

My paternal grandfather's name was Wong Gwong Cheung. He died in 1906 when I was only 3 or 4 years old. My grandmother's name was Lau. She had bound feet. She died in 1907 when I was 4 or 5 years old. My father had an older brother named Wong Kai. He did not have children. He died in 1908 when my brother and I were 6 and 7 years old.

My maternal grandfather was named Lau Sam. My maternal grandmother was named Choi. She had bound feet. They both died when I was very young, so I do not know much about them. My mother has an older brother named Lau Dak Man. According to my mother, he left home to go to Annam [Vietnam] when he was 17 or 18 years old. He has never returned and still lives in Annam. Today he is about 40 years old, married, and a father.

My house:

Our house is an old one, facing south. It is situated in the middle of the village. It is not near the sea but is about two Chinese miles from the sea at the county seat of Shek Kei. In front of the house is a field for crops. About one row of houses behind our house is a hill.

My house has two sections. It is about 18 feet in height and 64 feet in length. The middle section is about 12 feet wide.

The house has no side door, back door, indoor patio, or skylight. There is no fence, pavilion, garden, or backyard around the house. We never raised any domestic poultry around the house.

Glossary of Chinese Terms

Bing Kung Tong 秉公堂

Chong Chan 李應彬

Lincoln Chan 李采華

Steven Chan 嚴在民

Jack Chew 林值超

Chiuh Saan Plain 潮汕平原

Chong Ga Bin 張家邊

Chau Chow 周秋

Mrs. Joe Chow 何蘭清

Chungshan (Chung-shan) 中山

Chung wah wui gun (Chung-hua hui-kuan) 中華會館

Dai Leung 大良

dim sum 點心

Dung Chun 東村

fa-hung 花紅

Lum Bunn Fong 方林彬

gwoji teng 果子艇

Gwong Sang Cheung 廣生祥

Gwongtauh lou 光頭佬

Heungshan 香山
Houh Tauh 濠頭
Jan Ying Association 俊英工商會
Bob Jang 鄭榕森
Po Jang 鄭保
Jin Ying 志英
Joe Shoong 周崧
Joe Young 周忠泉
Alfred Jung 鄭慶饒
Kim Kee 建記
Kim Sang 建生
Kim Yick 建益
Hoy Kee 區開樞
Tom Chow King 周厚實
Lan Ting 蘭亭
Mrs. Jong Ho Leong 方婆婆
Ping Lee 簡治平
Joy Low 劉炳允
Ming Ma 馬林
So Yung Ng 吳壽容
Shek-Kei 石歧
(Chung-shan village)

Choi Sun 孫社才
Sum Sun 孫森
sun-fa kay 新花旗
Sze Yap 四邑
Gen. Tsai Teng Kai 蔡廷鍇
Toi Shan 台山
tongs 堂號
Joe Toy 蔡周
Tung Houh 東濠
Wah mok 華莫
wohng tong 黃糖
Yak ka! 吃啦
Yee Dai Ying 意大利
Yee Jee Ying 意志英
Wong Yow 黃有
yuan 圓
Yuen Fung 員峯

Selected Bibliography

Arreola, Daniel D. "Locke, California: Persistance and Change in the Curtural Landscape of a Delta Chinatown." Unpublished M.A. thesis, California State University at Hayward, 1975.

Augusta, Dorothy. "Locke." *Golden Notes,* v. 16, no. 4 (October 1970).

California Council for the Humanities (ed.). *American Chinatown: Pamphlet to accompany the Documentary.* San Francisco: California Council for the Humanities, 1982.

Chinn, Thomas H. Mark Lai, and Philip P. Choy (eds.), *A History of the Chinese in California: A Syllabus.* San Francisco: Chinese Historical Society of America, 1969.

Chiu, Ping *Chinese Labor in California, 1850-1880, an Economic Study.* Madison: University of Wisconsin, 1963.

Chu, George. "Chinatowns in the Delta: the Chinese in the Sacramento-San Joaquin Delta, 1870-1960," in *California Historical quarterly,* March 1970, v.47, n. 1.

Coolidge, Mary B. *Chinese Immigration.* 1909 reprint. New York: Arno Press, 1969.

Courtney, William J. *San Francisco's Anti-Chinese Ordinances, 1850-1900.* San Francisco: R and E Research Associates, 1974.

Delta Advisory Planning Council, "Delta Plan Technical Supplement" (Delta Historic Resources).

Hoexter, Corinne K. *From Canton to California: The Epic of Chinese Immigration.* New York: Four Winds Press, 1976.

Hom, Gloria Sun. *Chinese Argonauts: An Anthology of the Chinese Contribution to the Historical Development of Santa Clara County.* Los Altos: Foothill Community College, 1971.

Kingston, Maxine Hong. *China Men.* New York: Alfred A. Knopf, 1980.

Lee, Rose Hom. "The Decline of Chinatowns in the United States." *American Journal of Sociology,* v. 54, 1949.

Leung, Peter C.Y. "Wong Yow, A Chinese Farm Laborer in the Sacramento Delta." To appear in *California History* in 1984.

Leung, Peter, C.Y. and L. Eve Armentrout Ma. "Chinese and Commercial Agriculture in the Sacramento/San Joaquin Delta, 1910-1941." Unpublished article under consideration by *Pacific Historical Review.*

Loomis, A.E. "The Chinese as Agriculturalists." *Overland Monthly,* v. 4, 1870.

McGowan, Joseph A. *History of the Sacramento Valley.* New York: Lewis Historical Publishing Co., 1961.

Miller, Ronald D. and Peggy J. Miller. *Delta Country.* Glendale: La Siesta Press, 1971.

Ooms, Sally, "The Effects of Change and Intervention on the Chinese Town of Locke, California." Unpublished B.A. thesis, University of San Francisco, 1980.

Reed, Ann. "River Towns." *Sacramento Bee,* April 21, 1975.

Rossi, Jean. "Lee Bing, Founder of California's Historical Town of Locke." *The Pacific Historian,* v. 20, n. 4, 1976.

Sacramento Regional Area Planning Commission. "Regarding Locke State Historical Park."

Saxton, Alexander. *The Indispensible Enemy: Labor and the Anti-Chinese Movement in California.* Berkeley: University of California Press, 1971.

South China Morning Post. "Buying a Chunk of Chinese History." August 18, 1977.

Thompson, John. "The Settlement Geography of the Sacramento-San Joaquin Delta, California." Unpublished Ph.D. thesis, Stanford, University, 1957.

Trillin, Calvin, "U.S. Journal: Locke, California: The Last Chinatown." *New Yorker,* February 20, 1978, v. 54, n. 1.

Yip, Christopher. "Locke, California and the Chinese-Americans." Unpublished M.A. thesis, University of California at Berkeley, 1977.

Statements:
California Secretary of State March Fong Eu
and
California Senate Majority Leader John Garamendi

from California Secretary of State March Fong Eu:

Dear Mr. Leung:

Congratulations on the completion of your book, *One Day, One Dollar: Locke, California and the Chinese Farming Experience in the Delta.* It is a significant historical documentary on the bittersweet struggles of early Chinese immigrant farm laborers who toiled hard to make a living in this country. Moreover, you have been able to record for posterity their social and economic lives. This book, I feel, is a significant contribution to understanding the role of Chinese in the development of early California agriculture.

Sincerely,
March Fong Eu

from California Senate Majority Leader John Garamendi:

Dear Mr. Leung:

The written record of the Chinese immigrants in California's Delta is miniscule and hard to find. Their contributions, on the other hand, are large and readily apparent throughout meandering waterways and farmlands of the Delta. Your addition to the historical record fills a large gap and chronicles for all of us, Chinese and non-Chinese alike, the very important role these hardworking immigrants played in the settling of California.

Thank you for weaving more threads into the rich ethnic and cultural fabric of the Sacramento-San Joaquin Delta.

Sincerely,
John Garamendi

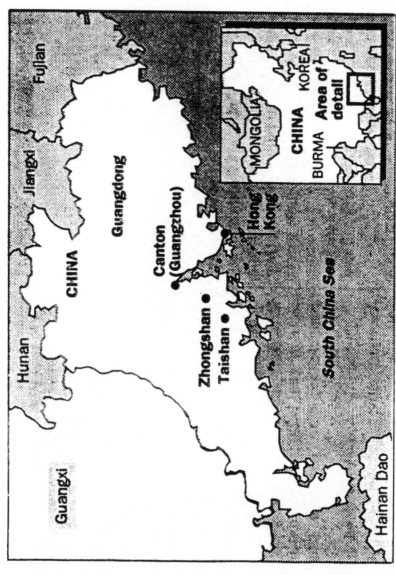

KWANGTUNG PROVINCE SHOWING MAJORITY CHINESE IMMIGRATED FROM ZHONGSHAN AND TAISHAN, AS WELL AS THEIR RELATED LOCATIONS TO CANTON, HONG KONG.

圖一 十九世紀大部份華工是來自廣東省的台山和中山縣一帶，圖示該縣與廣州、香港的位置。

Chungshan County is riddled with waterways from the delta.

圖二　珠江三角州中山縣的水道支流。

CHINESE FARMERS ON THEIR WAY TO THE FIELDS (CHUNGSHAN, CHINA).

圖三　中國中山縣的農作物到田間工作。

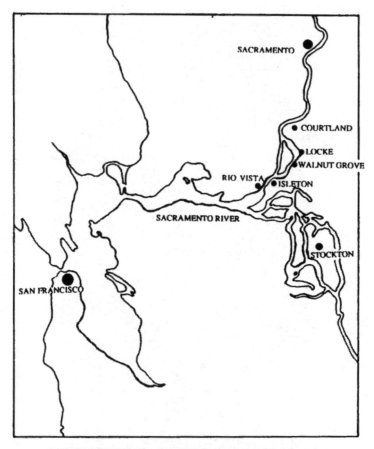

SAN FRANCISCO BAY and TOWNS IN THE SACRAMENTO DELTA
THAT HAVE CHINA TOWNS:

圖四　三藩市的海灣與在沙加緬度三角州建有唐人埠的城鎮：

SACRAMENTO	沙加緬度	COURTLAND	葛崙
LOCKE	樂居埠	WALNUT GROVE	汪古魯
ISLETON	埃靈頓	STOCKTON	市作頓
RIO VISTA	里奧威士打	SACRAMENTO RIVER	沙加緬度河
SAN FRANCISCO	三藩市		

Chinese levee builders on Sacramento River. 1896 drawing produced for *Overland Monthly*.

圖五　圖示一八九六年所繪的華人築堤工人工作情況。

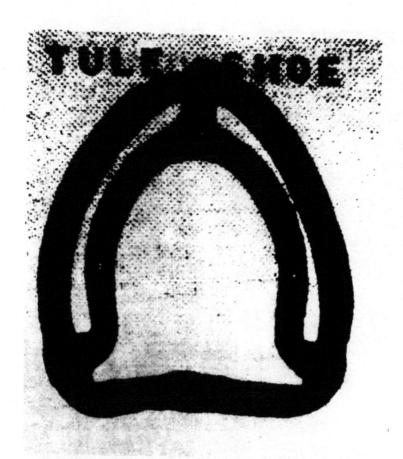

TULE SHOE: An oversized horseshoe, a devise created by the Chinese, was used in building levees in 1875's. THIS ORIGINAL TULE SHOE FOUND ON QUIMBY ISLAND IN 1942.

圖六　Tule Shoe(馬蹄鐵)：

圖片所示的馬蹄鐵於一九四二年由唐覺方特 (Thorkofod)在里奧威打床發掘出來。大約在一八 七五年中國人開始使用。鐵在馬鞋上，以防止在沼 澤工作的馬匹因過重而下陷。現存僅二個。

ISLETON'S CHINATOWN, CA. 1930.

圖八 一九三〇年埃靈頓的華埠。

88

This　　　　　is represntative of the basic tool used to build the first levees between 1860 and 1880. Its weight is 15 pounds.

圖七　Tule Cutter(切泥刀)：

這唯一的切泥刀爲當年華工築河堤所用的基本工具，是用來切泥塊，晒乾後爲河場泥磚，堆砌而成河堤的牆壁，該刀在一九八〇年由河床發掘出來，約十五磅重，現爲愛德華都拉所珍藏。

CHAUNCEY CHEW GENERAL MDSE. IN COUTLAND'S CHINATOWN. IT WAS BURNED DOWN IN 1937.

圖九　圖片葛崙華埠林燦士的商店一景。該華埠於一九三七年燒燬後便沒有重建。

BOARDED WALKWAY WITH CHINESE HOTEL, LOCKE, CA. 1930.
圖十　一九三〇年代樂居埠的中國旅店。

LOCKE VIEWED FROM THE SOUTH, NEAR THE RAILROAD TRACKS.
圖十一　　樂居埠的情景。

HUNDREDS OF BASKETS FULL OF PEACHES WERE TRANSPORTED WITH HORSES BY CHINESE TO THE RIVERBANK LANDING TO WAIT FOR STEAMERS TO SAN FRANCISCO, 1910.
圖十二　一九一〇年代三角州的園口收獲後，成千籮的桃
果放在河堤等着運送到三藩市之情景。

91

CHAUNCEY CHEW AND HIS WORKERS STANDING IN FRONT OF HIS ADVANCED
FARM EQUIPMENTS, 1910 s. 圖十三　一九一〇年代林燦士和他的園工站在他們
先進的農具前。

SING CHEW WAS A
TENANT FARMER
IN SOL RUNYON
RANCH, 1933.

圖十四
一九三三年林勝是
索林遜園的佃農。

92

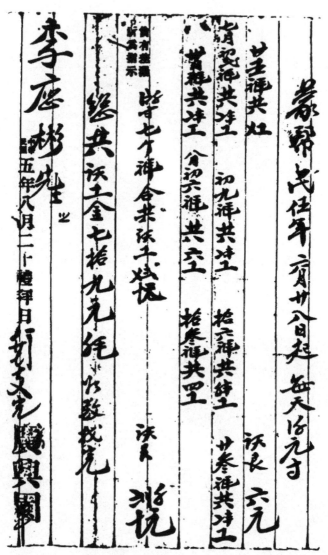

Payroll statement of Chong Chan issued by his uncle, a tenant farmer, on August 20, 1916. Chong Chan's salary started at $1.50 a day then was raised to $1.75 a day.

圖十五　一九一六年李應彬的工資文件，每天工資一元五角。

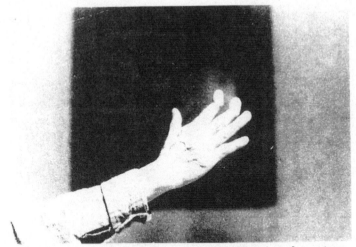

Farm laborer's fingers, deformed from extensive pruning of pear trees.
圖十六　由於終年累月的剪枝使其手部受害。

Farm laborer's hand showing skin damaged by pesticide.
圖十七　圖示農工手部所受殺蟲劑的影響。

WONG YOW (1900 - 1987), A CHINESE FARM LABOR
WORKING OVER FIFTY YEARS IN THE SACRAMENTO
RIVER DELTA.

圖十八　黃有在沙加緬度三角州一帶工
　　　　作了五十多年的農工。

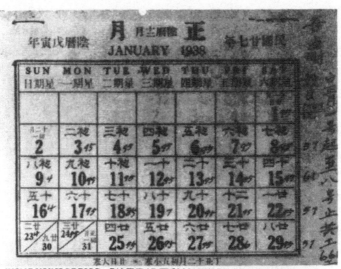

WONG YOW'S RECORD: CALENDAR FROM JANUARY OF 1938 SHOWING OF WORK AND RATE OF PAY-$0.30 AN HOUR.

圖十九　黃有用中國日曆記錄下一九三八年其工資和工作時間。

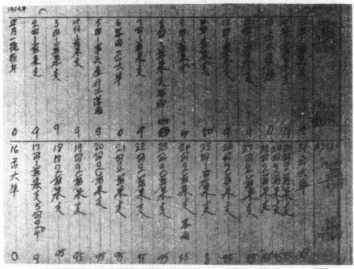

WONG YOW'S TIME SHEET (JANUARY, 1959) WHICH RECORDED DATES, LOCATIONS, HOURS AND TYPES OF WORK.

圖二十　黃有一九五九年的工作紀錄，指出日期、工作地點和工作種類。

96

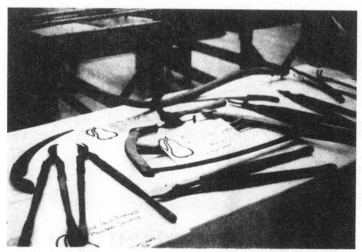

LINCOLN CHAN'S COLLECTION OF OLD PRUNING TOOLS USED BY CHINESE.

圖廿一　李朵華保留下的華人農工剪果枝的工具。

OLD PESTICIDE SPRAYING TOOLS.

圖廿二　舊式的噴射果樹竹桿。

BRANCH OF KOUMINTANG (KMT, CHINESE NATIONALIST PARTY) IN
COURTLAND'S CHINATOWN, 1920's.

圖廿三　一九二〇年代葛崙華埠國民黨支部。

STUDENTS AND TEACHERS' PICNIC FROM COURTLAND'S CHINESE
LANGUAGE SCHOOL, 1930'S.

　　圖廿四　一九三〇年代葛崙華文學師生郊遊留影。

CHINESE LOTTERY TICKET(PAK-KOP PIU) FROM LOCKE SHOWING DRAWING TIMES.

圖廿五　樂居鎮賭館的白鴿票據，註明一天開彩兩次的時間。

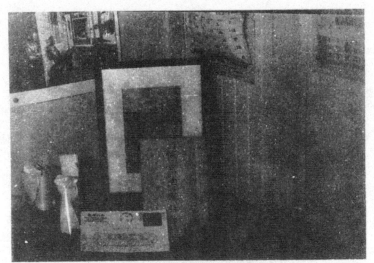

THE HAPPY READING CLUB IN LOCKE, 1979.
圖廿六　一九七九年樂居鎮的快樂報社。

MRS. TIN HOOK LEE AND HER HUSBAND WERE TENANT FARMERS IN
HOOD, CLASKBURG, AND STEAMBOAT SLOUGH UNTIL 1937. SHE HAD
TO PREPARE MEALS FOR LABORERS WHO WORKED IN HER ORCHARD.
THIS PICTURE SHOWS HER WITH HER FOUR CHILDREN IN 1933.
圖廿七　李天福春婦在三角州一帶做佃農做到一九三七年。
　　　　李天福夫人除了爲農煮食外，還要照顧她的兒女。